"Raising Gifted Kids is essential reading for every parent who has a gifted child. Many books address gifted kids' educational issues, but *Raising Gifted Kids* also warns you about and helps you avoid the emotional traps of stress, anxiety, perfectionism, and burnout. A must-have for every parent who wants to help their child reach his or her potential— happily!"

—Professor Lynn A. Stout, UCLA School of Law

"Dr. Klein's book provides valuable insights for parents and teachers of gifted children, who present unique and sometimes daunting challenges for parents and teachers. Their gifts come with complications and responsibilities. Think of this book as the manual you need to help your child thrive."

—Gary A. Carnow, Ed.D, Director, Technology and Information Services, Alhambra Unified School District

"Parents of gifted children are barraged with information about how to best approach the challenges of meeting their child's unique needs. As a parent of a gifted child, I found that very few experts addressed the substance of what Dr. Barbara Klein makes a point to discuss in her new book: the emotional development of the gifted child. I believe that finding the best resources for educating gifted children is very important. But I also believe that preparing gifted children for living in the larger world is the best gift parents and educators can give them. Dr. Klein understands that these are still children, after all, and that their intellects will be best served by attending to the whole child. I highly recommend this book to all parents searching for tools and insight into how best to serve their gifted children."

—Julie Bergman Sender, mother of Emily, age 8

"Reading Dr. Barbara Klein's book is like having a wise and caring personal guide through the challenges and joys of raising a gifted child. She provides both the realism and optimism we need to help our children define and fulfill their dreams."

—Carolyn McWilliams, M.A., Founder, Bridges Academy; Educational Consultant

"Barbara Klein delivers a comprehensive, hands-on approach to parenting the gifted child. She brings a passion to the subject and provides insightful tips on parenting these unique children."

—Paul Cummins, Founder, Crossroads School, Santa Monica;
Executive Director, New Visions Foundation, Santa Monica

"Dr. Klein's clinical interactions with gifted children and their parents indicate that with gifted kids, it's "good enough" parenting that works best. Alternatively, both perfectionistic and negligent parenting styles will have destructive effects on the children's development."

—John Sutton, Ed.D., Executive Coordinator,
UCLA Academic Preparation & Educational Partnership Programs

Raising Gifted Kids

Other Books by the Author

Klein, B.S. *Not All Twins Are Alike: Psychological Profiles of Twinship.* Praeger Publishers, Westport, CT, 2003.

Schave, B. *Forgotten Memories: A Journey Out of the Darkness of Sexual Abuse.* Praeger Publishers, New York, NY, 1993.

Schave, D., and B. Schave. *Early Adolescence and the Search for Self: A Developmental Perspective.* Praeger Publishers, New York, NY, 1989.

McNeil, J.D., and B. Schave. *Issues in School Reform: A View from the Bottom Up.* Optimization Software, New York, NY, 1985.

Wulf, K., and B. Schave. *Curriculum Design: A Handbook for Educators.* Scott Foresman, Chicago, IL, 1983.

Schave, B., and J. Ciriello. *Identity and Intimacy in Twins.* Praeger Publishers, New York, NY, 1983.

Raising Gifted Kids

Everything You Need to Know to Help Your
Exceptional Child Thrive

Barbara Klein, Ph.D.

American Management Association

New York • Atlanta • Brussels • Chicago • Mexico City • San Francisco
Shanghai • Tokyo • Toronto • Washington, D.C.

Special discounts on bulk quantities of AMACOM books
are available to corporations, professional associations,
and other organizations. For details, contact
Special Sales Department, AMACOM, a division of
American Management Association,
1601 Broadway, New York, NY 10019.
Tel.: 212-903-8316.   Fax: 212-903-8083.
Web Site: www.amacombooks.org

This publication is designed to provide accurate and authoritative
information in regard to the subject matter covered. It is sold with
the understanding that the publisher is not engaged in rendering
legal, accounting, or other professional service. If legal advice or
other expert assistance is required, the services of a competent professional person should be sought.

The names of the participants in this book have been changed to
protect their privacy. Places referred to have also been changed for
reasons of confidentiality.

Library of Congress Cataloging-in-Publication Data

Klein, Barbara Schave.
   Raising gifted kids : everything you need to know to help your exceptional
child thrive / Barbara Klein.
       p.   cm.
   Includes bibliographical references and index.
   ISBN-13: 978-0-8144-7342-9
   ISBN-10: 0-8144-7342-3
   1. Gifted children.   2. Child rearing.   3. Parenting.   4. Parent and child.
   I. Title.

   HQ773.5.K54   2007
   649'.155—dc22

                                                            2006019904

Printing number

10   9   8   7   6   5   4   3   2

Contents

Foreword

Raising Gifted Kids: Everything You Need to Know to Help Your Exceptional Child Thrive is more than a practical cookbook in the interest of better parenting of gifted children. In addition to learning from firsthand accounts by children and their parents as they confront and overcome obstacles to the development of their potential, the reader will become knowledgeable in the scholarship of giftedness, how to acquire effective ways to enhance giftedness in the home, and how to negotiate learning opportunities in school and other institutions on behalf of the gifted child.

Raising Gifted Kids departs from the prevailing educational policy of "dumbing down" and restricting learning opportunities to the "one-size-fits-all" philosophy in the guise of equality and social justice. Instead, Dr. Barbara Klein documents the great ranges in talent and human potential, while showing what it takes to develop individual capacities that will best serve society. Readers of this book will become more aware of the many ways we (parents, teachers, schools, and society at large) are shortchanging our gifted children, at great cost to ourselves.

There is another important reason for reading this book. The United States is in the throes of a great cultural conflict regarding who should have responsibility for the educational development of the child. Debate is raging over charter schools, judging schools by results of mandated test scores, required preschooling, and education in the home. In her interesting and insightful presentation, Dr. Klein reveals factors often overlooked in discussing these issues and equips the reader for fruitful participation in deciding how best to educate children who have widely different potentials.

At a time when polarization in education is tending toward external control of the child, *Raising Gifted Kids* offers practical ways for parents to exercise their responsibility and power to make their voices heard. In trying to correct this imbalance, Dr. Klein believes that parents can and should be the key players in decisions regarding the education of their children.

In brief, the author delivers more than meets the eye. Parents and teachers will find insights, practices, and inspiration that are grounded in the best of what knowledge and experience have to offer. What's more, the reader will find the stories engaging and personally relevant.

As one who has been professionally occupied in education for many years and with the opportunity to know Dr. Klein and her work with children and parents, I attest to the validity of her recommendations. She is a teacher in the best sense, and one in which parents and children can place their trust.

John D. McNeil
Professor of Education Emeritus
University of California, Los Angeles

Acknowledgments

I have been fortunate to have the insights and support of many talented individuals as I worked on this book. First, I thank Paul Macirowski for inspiring, motivating, and helping me with every aspect of this project. Paul reviewed and edited my manuscript, bringing everything into sharper focus for my readers. Dr. John McNeil, my dear friend, was an extravagant resource who was always available to consult, edit, and clarify my ideas. My personal assistant, Joelle Oviatt, was instrumental in the production of this book. She worked tirelessly typing, retyping, and—most miraculously—deciphering my handwriting. Al Zuckerman and his assistant Maya Rock at Writers House were a cornerstone of the project. Al "got" my message and helped develop it into this book, and Maya was willing and able to help translate Al's many ideas. I am grateful for their understanding. Thank you, Ellen Kadin at AMACOM, for taking a chance.

The mothers and fathers who attended my parenting groups are a vital part of this book. These parents are generous of spirit, and I thank them for their support. They asked to remain anonymous so I changed their names in the text to protect their privacy. The gifted children I have known are also a cornerstone of this work, and I am grateful that they shared their thoughts and feelings with me.

Finally, every time I write a book, I thank my children and, now, also their spouses, for being patient, encouraging, thoughtful, and honest: Elizabeth, Jonathan, Richard, and Kim. I am truly fortunate to have such gifted children, who inspire me to be the best I can be.

Raising Gifted Kids

The Parent's Dilemma

This is truly an exciting time to be working in the field of child development. I enthusiastically believe that times have changed for
the betterment of our children. Educators and psychologists know
more about child development and how to apply their knowledge
to answering questions such as: What helps children develop into
self-actualized and productive members of society? What types of
experiences prevent children from realizing their potential? What
are the critical time periods for intervention? What types of intervention give results? Now we have answers.

In a real sense, we can now see that parents are more important than ever because research has demonstrated their power and
influence. We now know with great certainty the significance of appropriate parenting in the child's development. When children are
treated with proper attention and care, they have a chance of finding their true passions, developing meaningful lives, and contributing to their chosen community. Children who do not receive

1

appropriate parenting or are left to their own devices are not as fortunate, and they have a much harder time finding their identity in our often troubled and chaotic world.

Parents can no longer take their role lightly. You know that what you do for your children will have an impact. While previous generations felt comfortable following the old rules of parenting or abdicating their responsibility for parenting to others, this generation has been informed by their own education and the popular press that they must take charge of their decision making to be effective.

As a parent today, knowledge is your power base. The continuing desire to learn and do the best you can for your child is your hope and reward. Parenting is a challenge for all parents. But parents of gifted children face more challenges and have a greater opportunity to raise children who will really make a difference to our complicated modern world. Specifically, you face serious challenges helping develop your gifted child's potential.

Educational Challenges

Educational opportunities for gifted children are—at best—hard to find, uninviting, or boring. At worst, they are poorly organized or even disastrous. Extremely precocious children who are highly sensitive, curious, and mature far beyond their ages may be easily misunderstood and poorly educated by the schools they attend. Our society bears a subtle but real anti-intellectual bias against extremely bright children, labeling them "intense," "demanding," "misfits," "nerds," and "eggheads." The sad result is that gifted children are not encouraged to develop a unique self-awareness or to further their special potential in mathematics, science, writing, music, technology, or art.

Strange as it may seem, many parents of gifted children are unaware of or indifferent to the importance of utilizing and advancing their child's gift. Many parents don't know how to challenge their children to use their analytic, interpersonal, musical, mathematical, or creative skills. Extremely talented kids need to be given opportunities to solve unique problems, to share their insights, and to create music, poetry, drama, or art that is way beyond what might be expected of a normal child.

There is little room for the gifted student in today's schools, which focus on the noble but unfair mantra of "equality for all learners," where bland sameness substitutes for true equality. Confined to unchallenging curriculum and learning experiences, gifted children immediately suffer from serious boredom. In sharp contrast, your gifted children will soar if they are given tasks that require demanding learning challenges.

Caring and informed parents can become frustrated with the bureaucracies of public and private schools. Nearly every school has metaphorically built a fortress to keep all parents, whether helpful or destructive, out of policy making and curriculum design. Parents who want a voice in their children's schooling don't know how to get administrators and teachers to respond to the special needs of the gifted child.

Two Cautionary Tales

Gifted children's responses to unsatisfying educational situations can take many forms. Here are two cautionary examples, from the many available, to illustrate the point.

Let's examine the misadventures of Annie, whose first-grade teacher suspects giftedness because of her curiosity and ability to respond quickly in class. The school psychologist gives Annie an IQ test protocol. Annie scores in the gifted range (above 132) and is placed in a highly competitive program with a narrow focus on academics. Highly perfectionist by nature, Annie is encouraged to compete with other gifted children and become a wiz kid. There is little concern for the negative aftereffects of high parental and teacher expectations, such as depression or burnout for the pressured gifted child. Rather, the stereotypical belief that all gifted children do well under pressure is used as the primary educational intervention at home and at school.

In school and other social situations, Annie is sometimes treated as if she is normal and like other children and at other times as if she is a weird genius. At best, superficial attempts—such as labeling her as gifted or putting her in "pull-out" classes—are made to deal with her unique cognitive and personality development. By the time she graduates high school, Annie has experienced depression, academic burnout, and acting out with drugs and promiscuous sexuality, all because the pressure has been too much for her to handle. Annie has never developed a realistic sense of herself. She can be very driven or very down on herself.

When Annie finally seeks help in a mental health professional's office, it is too late to redeem her academic career. Her grades are so terrible that she won't be admitted to her top college choices. Annie believes that she is nothing if she is not on top. As an older adolescent and young adult, Annie will struggle to find her true passion and what is meaningful to her in life.

Now consider an opposite example, Shelley, who has believed from the very early age of five that her intelligence makes her unpopular. She does not want to be a social outcast. Shelley dumbs herself down. She stays away from her true passions and lives out her fantasy of being the prom queen. She seeks out the most successful teenage boy at her high school and tries to find happiness supporting her boyfriend and eventual husband.

Unfortunately for Shelley, her husband is not appreciative of her efforts to be his partner. He is not honest and betrays her. Eventually, they divorce. Shelley becomes vulnerable to serious depression and suicide, in part because she has not developed her own talents or even acknowledged her own self-worth. Shelley struggles as an adult to find her true self and to make her life meaningful.

Other gifted children have less dramatic but equally insidious problems to deal with as they search to find a place where they shine. Sometimes they are teased or bullied. They can be used by other children and teachers because they are smart and talented. Very often, they are treated as social misfits and they become isolated, leading to loneliness and despair.

Academic problems also occur. Gifted children are not always "A" students because of asynchronous development, uneven and unpredictable learning styles, their intense need to be perfect, their boredom with the subject matter, or their fears of competition, which are closely related to their perfectionism.

How I've Learned About Gifted Children

So you may be wondering where my strong ideas, opinions, and feelings about gifted children come from. They are hard won from my own personal and professional life experiences. I grew up in a gifted family, with a highly gifted older brother who graduated from Cal Tech at 21 with a Ph.D. in astrophysics and a moderately gifted twin sister who now teaches at Stanford. I had the pleasure of raising two highly gifted children in the 1970s and 1980s. While raising my children, I earned a master's and doctorate in early childhood education and a second doctorate in clinical psychology. I worked as a psychotherapist and school consultant for more than 20 years with families who had gifted children. For many years I worked with private and public schools for gifted children in Southern California. I consulted with many parents of gifted children, along with the children themselves. And these gifted children began to teach me about their issues with their parents, their friends, and at school.

Given my deep concerns about the intellectual and emotional needs of gifted children, and armed with my knowledge of the field, I began to focus on how best to help gifted children and their families. I started a parenting education and support group for parents of gifted children. I knew from my own experiences as a mother and from my countless serious conversations with parents of gifted children that families felt isolated. There was no one to compare notes with on the crucial major decision questions as well as the day-to-day issues involved in parenting. To make matters worse, nongifted parents felt that the problems of the parents of gifted children were ridiculous. They were jealous, unempathetic, and even mean to the mothers who had talented children. "Gifted children can raise themselves," was the common refrain of uninformed parents with nongifted children when offering advice to the mothers and fathers who consulted with me.

Being somewhat passionate and driven myself about what is in a child's best interests, I began my new adventure of helping parents learn more about gifted children than their IQ scores. In the process I unearthed many very compelling psychological truths. I discovered that mothers of gifted children had some strikingly similar issues with their own children, as well as unique problems that related to their family structure and the need for the mother to work. On the one hand, when mothers had to work to contribute to the family income, the quality of their parenting was affected adversely. On the other hand, mothers who stayed home with their children could become too indulgent and wrapped up in their child's problems. I saw firsthand the negative consequences of *helicopter parenting*.

I found out that I was right about the need for friendship and support for parents of gifted children. Every mother or father who came to my group was deeply relieved to know that other parents had similar problems with their gifted children. All of these parents felt that being in my education and support group helped them to be more effective parents. These parents became more aware of and concerned with their child's unique intellectual and emotional needs. They did not feel that it was necessary for their child to attend a gifted school, although some parents chose to do so.

Through a group process, those parents who attended developed a heightened self-awareness of their reactions to their children. I worked with my group members on understanding the concept of overidentification with their child. The dangers of perfectionism with gifted children was belabored, some would say, in my parenting group. Mothers and fathers learned to avoid putting pressure on their children in terms of achievement or social expectations. They became mindful of their child's need to be challenged in a unique way. They resolved that they would try to accept the burdens as well as the special attention they received because their child is gifted. They learned they did not have to be the perfect parent they had imagined.

I learned that individually and as a group, parents of gifted children wanted their voices to be heard by other parents, teachers, and schools. They were extremely eager to do the best job they could as mothers and fathers. They learned not to take no for an answer, be it from a school, their spouse, or even from me. They came to my group to get my ideas and the ideas of the other group members in order to make the best possible decisions about parenting their children.

What This Book Will Do for You

You've probably figured out by now that the members of my group of parents of gifted children are gifted themselves and are single-minded. My group members believe that there is a right way to parent a highly gifted child and there is a wrong way. With their support and concerns, I am writing this book to share some of my own theories, ideas, and insights into raising a gifted child. Included, as well, are my group members' individual insights into parenting their gifted children. Interlaced throughout will be my reactions to dealing with both the gifted parents of gifted children and to dealing with the children themselves.

I ask that you be open-minded to my insight-oriented, psycho-dynamic perspective, which is an introspective approach rooted in both my personal and professional experiences, and which helps parents understand how unresolved emotional issues from the past, i.e., childhood, can affect parenting decisions in the present. My philosophy is hard-won and based on many triumphs. My mistakes have been informative as well.

Although there are many fine books about gifted children, they merely describe the phenomenon or characteristics of giftedness (beyond a score on an IQ test), and then suggest some prescriptive steps, which include advocating and standing up for your gifted child. I wholeheartedly believe that you must advocate for your gifted child, but how do you really become an advocate and not another pushy parent?

My book goes further and presents the ongoing emotional struggles of parents trying to raise their gifted child. It also presents the emotional struggles and triumphs of the gifted child growing up in an anti-intellectual, consumer-driven, fragmented, technological society. The real voices of parents and children informing us of their joy, pain, disappointment, and confusion add a new, emotionally honest dimension to understanding giftedness. These life stories of mothers and fathers trying to parent the right way for their gifted child will add insight into the depth of the problem. In addition, readers will learn new strategies for dealing with their little darlings.

I hope my book will provoke you to think about your own childhood and how your memories and experiences are affecting your parenting style. I am convinced that childhood experiences strongly determine parental motivation. Thinking about your own frame of reference as a parent—how your parents or caregivers raised you—will help you to react more objectively to your child. For example, giving your child what you didn't get will not make you a good parent. You need to understand why you are giving or not giving to your child.

I believe the many anecdotes, case histories, and parental advisories will stimulate your own creativity and capacity to find new solutions to your children's developmental needs. Problems you currently have—with the right school placement, social and separation anxiety, perfectionism, under- or overachievement—are just a few of the difficulties that will be tackled. Your gifted child will appear to be happier and more relaxed when you finish reading. And you, my readers, will feel challenged, but informed and capable of success.

CHAPTER ONE

Is My Child Really Gifted?

Have you ever wondered if your child is gifted? Then the advice of child development experts finally registers on your radar screen. Or perhaps you have just been told that your child is gifted as measured on a standardized IQ test. Whether you already suspected this or not, finding out that your child is gifted can give rise to some immediate questions and concerns. What do you do now? Do you have to start looking for special programs or a special school for your little genius? Will your child be labeled as a geek or a nerd and never fit in socially with his or her peers? What impact will this have on your other children, especially if they are not as gifted?

Certain parents are overjoyed at this news. They consider their child to be a new status symbol, an accessory to their own brilliance. Other parents are in denial. They decide that this unwelcome information can and should be ignored, or at least taken lightly in relationship to other family issues. And still others recognize that they have been given an enormous responsibility and they want to do the best job of being a parent that is humanly possible. I hope you fall into this last category.

Understanding Giftedness

Before anything else, you must try to understand what it means that your child is gifted. This can be a difficult task for countless reasons, but two stand out:

1. There is no agreed-upon definition of the qualities of intellect and personality necessary to categorize a child as gifted.
2. There are many powerful and confusing myths in our society about gifted children and adults.

Both reasons are huge factors in why it is often difficult to recognize and understand gifted children. Let's look at each reason in a little more detail.

Measuring Giftedness

IQ is often used as the basic measure for giftedness. The most common standardized tests used on an individual basis to measure intelligence are the Stanford-Binet Intelligence Test and the Wechsler Scales of Intelligence. IQ scores between 132 and 145 are considered in the gifted range: the 98th percentile in a statistical sample. Scores above 145 are considered in the high gifted range: the 99th percentile in a statistical sample.

The Stanford-Binet and the Wechsler Scales are used to measure general intellectual abilities. But many practical professionals who work with children think that there should be a way to test for multiple intelligences, a more refined and diverse theory of intelligence. They are looking for a definition of giftedness that will apply to all children in all areas of intellectual, musical, scientific, or artistic endeavor. Obviously, musical talent differs from mathematical talent, which differs from abstract reasoning and the ability to express oneself in writing or speaking. Unequivocally, there is no one-size-fits-all definition that can be used to describe the gifted child.

Dispelling Myths About Giftedness

Myths about giftedness permeate our culture. The prevalence of these myths can result in a variety of problems for you as the parent of a gifted child and for your child. Among the most common myths are the following:

- ❑ "Every child is gifted."
- ❑ "Gifted children are easy to raise."
- ❑ "Gifted children are nerds and geeks."
- ❑ "Gifted children are strangely manipulative and grow up to be white-collar criminals."
- ❑ "Gifted children are so intensely emotional that they cannot exist in the real world. Often they commit suicide because they feel so tortured."

Society flourishes and moves forward because of individuals who have a vision, genius, or talent that enhances or improves our understanding of ourselves and of the world. To create a context where this can happen, it is imperative that talent, creativity, and genius be discovered and nurtured in our children. Schooling and the understanding of child development are the keys to developing gifted potential. Unfortunately, gifted education is neglected. The development of gifted children puzzles and concerns parents, educators, psychologists, and other mental health professionals.

General confusion about which children are really gifted stems from both the prevalent myths and the fact that there is no working definition of giftedness. Clearly, and unequivocally, giftedness is today misunderstood and misused as a psychological and educational construct by parents and educators.

A General Definition of Giftedness

Since psychology became recognized as a science in the 1850s, psychologists have tried to demonstrate the existence of giftedness as a psychological phenomenon. Researchers have used twin studies for more than 150 years to prove that giftedness not only exists, but that intellectual potential is genetically determined. Although there have been flaws in this genetic research, there are nonetheless conclusive indications that intellectual potential has roots in the child's genetic endowment. Culture, environment, and parenting contribute significantly to the giftedness laid down in the child's genetic makeup.

Just as researchers disagree about what makes a child gifted, so do parents and educators. When I talk to persuasive and positive parents, I can totally understand why some have difficulty getting a grip on what is distinctive about a gifted child. The following conversation illustrates the confusion that many have concerning gifted children. Linda is a successful actress and a gifted mother in my group for parents of gifted children.

"Linda," I say in a serious voice, "the statistical likelihood of having a gifted child is pretty small. The odds are obviously even much higher against having a highly gifted child. How could it be possible that so many mothers think their children are gifted?"

Linda, who has an extremely large network of friends and acquaintances, replies, as she always does, in an enthusiastic tone, "I know it is hard to believe, but honestly, Barbara, I have never met a mother who didn't think her child belonged at the local school for the highly gifted. No, wait a second, I'm wrong. I know a mother of triplets. She thinks that the nonidentical triplet is not as gifted as the two identical ones. But most mothers think their child is gifted, or will be gifted if they get the right tutoring."

The part of myself that is steeped in academic knowledge cannot believe what Linda is saying. Only the top 2 percent of all children on the bell curve qualify as gifted, while only 1 in 100 is considered highly gifted. But another part of me, the "grandmom about town," knows that her words have a ring of truth if you hear them through the perspective of positive or naive parents.

Why do most parents want to believe that their child or children are gifted? This leap of faith is natural, healthy, and well-meaning. Parents should believe in their children. From a psychological perspective, our children represent our hopes and dreams. By believing in your child you are in essence believing in yourself and your capacity to create and to nurture. Effective parents will, at different times, see their son or daughter as talented, capable, brilliant, charming, and able to accomplish anything he or she wants to do.

And yet, because I have talked with and evaluated many gifted children, I must stick to the reality, and not the fantasy. Hoping or believing that your child is gifted is a far cry from the actuality of trying to raise a gifted son or daughter. Raising a gifted or highly gifted child is entirely different from raising a child who is bright and high-achieving, or who is normal, or who has learning problems or special needs, because of each gifted child's unique personality and learning style.

Another gifted mother, an articulate law professor in my parenting group, likened trying to raise a highly gifted child to her experience of figuring out how to drive a high-performance car with the wrong owner's manual. Janice advises, "You need to get the right owner's manual for parenting highly gifted children. You've got a different model of child from most parents, so you will need different parenting instructions to be a good parent. If you try and follow the standard instructions, you're going to push the lever you think turns on the lights and get the windshield wipers instead."

Characteristic Behaviors of Gifted Children

Whether or not giftedness can be precisely measured in its entirety, parents, psychologists, and educators know that it is an actual phenomenon that exists as part of an individual's personality. There are lists of behavioral characteristics of gifted children available to help parents and educators to understand how to assess giftedness.

As already mentioned, characteristics of gifted children include, but are not limited to, an IQ of more than 132 (above 145 for highly gifted) on the standard intelligence tests. Characteristics of the gifted or highly gifted may also include children with musical or artistic gifts way beyond their chronological age, children who demonstrate an extreme capacity for creative or divergent thinking, or children who are psychological insightful or socially responsible with leadership abilities.

Professor of psychology professor Ellen Winner (*Gifted Children: Myths and Realities*, Basic Books, 1996) defines three atypical characteristics of gifted children that go beyond a measurement on an IQ test:

1. Gifted children are precocious and learn more quickly and easily than typical children.
2. Gifted children insist on marching to their own drummer, which includes the ability to learn quickly on their own, and the ability to make up rules as they go along. Very smart children solve problems in novel and idiosyncratic ways.
3. Gifted children have a strong desire for mastery. They are intrinsically motivated to make sense of the domain in which they show precocity, which often includes an obsessive and sharp focus on their own interests.

Chapter 4 describes in detail characteristic behaviors that I see as defining giftedness. In brief, gifted children are critical thinkers; creative, rapid learners; curious; capable of being highly communicative; extremely perceptive; able to retain information easily; and committed to a task, which they pursue resourcefully and in detail. Gifted children also are highly sensitive. In situations where they feel out of place or misunderstood, gifted children can act in highly anxious or in other emotional ways. Very smart children may have socialization problems and feel awkward because of their intellectual superiority in comparison to their peer group. Gifted children are often treated as strange by other children because they are so smart.

One important, and difficult, characteristic I have encountered and observed many times over with gifted children and their parents is perfectionism. Parents of extremely smart children are usually extremely smart as well. If they are involved with their children, parents want only the "best" for every child-rearing situation. This intensity can create another layer of difficulty or stress for both the parent and the child in day-to-day relations. The sense of urgency and entitlement that everything must be accomplished according to high standards leads me to conclude that most gifted parents tend to be perfectionists who overidentify with their children. Very bright parents may have unrealistic expectations for themselves and their children. This is definitely something to watch out for and try to avoid.

By contrast, parents who are mature and sufficiently satisfied with their own lives are better able to help their children to develop their own inner talents and identity. Parents who have some insight into themselves and their children focus on realistic problems to promote their child's potential instead of creating or helping to create anxiety, depression, or burnout.

Education for the Gifted Child

The challenge of educating a bright child is substantial. Parents understandably look to schools for help with their children's education. Unfortunately, most schools are not prepared to work with either the observable or latent potential of gifted children. My serious concern is that gifted children have been ignored and neglected by the trend toward equality for all children that is currently prevalent in education. The "No Child Left Behind" Act of 2001 provides no incentive for schools to attend to the growth of students once they attain proficiency. Because educators have not developed programs for the gifted, we are falling behind as a nation in many areas. The United States no longer has the finest scientists, technological wizards, entrepreneurial managers, or artists. I am sure America can do much better.

As an advocate for gifted children, I have spoken with countless principals, directors of admissions, and teachers who are tired of hearing every parent claim that his or her child is gifted. They seem annoyed or bored or indifferent to the problem of gifted children and their families. Their ignorance or indifference makes the problem of raising a gifted child even more difficult and puzzling. I conclude that the majority of educators don't want to deal with the extra problems that are created by gifted children. I can see that very few public schools have made real accommodations for the gifted child. Private schools who work with gifted children can also fall short because they fail to take into account the emotional and social needs of extremely bright children. And unfortunately, both private and public schools ignore the creative aspects of giftedness.

Parents of gifted children are stressed further because they are often isolated from the normal interactions between parents and teachers, which serve to provide direction, insight, and support about how to parent. Angela, a highly gifted mother and stellar financial manager in my parenting group, echoes my feeling about the alienation of the parent of a gifted child. Angela says: "Work with the teachers to help them understand your child. Don't complain to other parents that you have special challenges because your child is gifted. Other parents will not appreciate this information.

And they may actually use it against you and your child by making you feel strange and outcast."

Janice, the law professor, states, "The hardest thing about being a parent of a gifted child is relative isolation—their problems and mine seem so different from those of other children and parents. As a consequence it is hard to find understanding and guidance from other parents and even from many professionals. It is also easy to feel as if either my child is abnormal (defective) or I am an abnormal (defective) mother."

Developing Your Gifted Child's Potential

As a parent, your reaction to having a gifted child and your plan of action going forward is the most crucial part of the child's educational, social, and emotional development. The lack of educational support for parents of gifted children, coupled with the general misunderstanding about what it means to be gifted, leaves you out in the cold making decisions about what to do to help your child grow up and flourish. You want your gifted children to be properly educated, in touch with their passions, and able to interact with others comfortably. Without any kind of meaningful support, this parenting task is quite hard to accomplish. You clearly need help!

From my counseling, consulting, and teaching experiences, I know that parents of highly gifted children sense deep down that their infant or toddler is very advanced, but they are often unsure about what they should do with this awareness, other than talk to other parents and their own parents. Indeed, parents of highly gifted children have very complicated reactions to the news that their child is in the 99th percentile. This tidbit of crucial, objective information can come from different sources. Indeed, the information the IQ score provides is objective; reactions to it are decidedly not. Most commonly, the bombshell is dropped on a mother or father by a caring teacher, a trusted pediatrician, or a relative stranger such as a mental health professional. Psychologists, psy-chiatrists, and psychoanalysts often come in contact with gifted children because the gifted tend to be extremely emotional and may be having behavioral problems at school or home.

Even though parents know intuitively that their child is gifted, they have very distinctive reaction patterns when facing their unique situation and challenges head on. From my experiences eval-uating hundreds of children, three types of very different parental reaction patterns are common:

1. Parents who are overly enthusiastic—just plain delighted to be told that there is giftedness in the family. This pro-vides them with a new status symbol, another accessory to indicate their brilliance and power.

2. The family who is living in denial and chooses to ignore the unwanted information that their child is gifted. For this family, other overriding family issues or values shove the issue of giftedness to the back burner.

3. The most adaptive reaction is the concerned parent who is able to realize that he or she has been given a huge re-sponsibility. Concerned parents want to do the best job of being a parent within the limits of their abilities. You already know that I wholeheartedly recommend the third approach.

Parental Reactions to Raising a Gifted Child

Let's look at some case examples that illustrate my point that par-ents' reactions and plans of action for their gifted child are crucial factors in the child's development.

The Accessory Parent

The *accessory parent* is my shorthand code for those parents who don't see the "whole" responsibility and inherent problem of raising a gifted child because of their own immaturity and unresolved narcissistic needs for admiration. Accessory parents are delighted that they have a little prodigy or genius because it reflects well on them and their intellectual, creative, or artistic strengths. Their child is used as a status symbol, an accessory to their identity as a brilliant parent.

You can easily pick out these overly proud parents. These are the ones at a cocktail party or a parent–teacher meeting who let you know their son's or daughter's IQ score. It doesn't matter what your interest level is in their child's brilliance—you are going to know in five minutes that their son has a 140 IQ. These parents talk uncontrollably about their children's talents because they crave the attention they get from others.

Bragging about their very smart children to strangers is a mistake, but some parents don't know any better. I don't think their intentions are sinister: I believe that accessory parents see *everything* in life as a potential status symbol. Undoubtedly, these parents are living through their child's giftedness. They do not realize the damage that they are doing to their child's identity development and future happiness. By treating their children as if they are an item in their portfolio of accomplishments, they marginalize their children's well-being. Unfortunately, parents like this often find out later in life how damaging it was to treat their child as an asset when the child is demonstrating such self-destructive behavior as drug addiction, anorexia, or suicide attempts.

Usually I work very briefly with overly proud parents, because they are not especially interested in gaining knowledge or insight into their child. But they are extremely involved in the IQ score that is attained on a standardized test. When their children "make the cut," they are eager to immediately place them into a status-oriented and competitive gifted program in a public or private school. Or they may promote their children in a different but equally competitive way. For example, accessory parents often relentlessly push their children to be the smartest, the best of the best in their area of talent and in life.

These parents don't give their children the love and emotional support they need. The motivation to understand what is unique about their children is certainly not essential to these status-conscious uninformed people. Overly proud parents prefer to delegate responsibility for their children to teachers and to schools. If these parents are wealthy, they will spend inordinate amounts of money on lessons and tutoring for their child. They will focus on developing perfection in their children—who are by nature perfectionists and really don't need further encouragement. Children with very narcissistic accessory parents may grow up with an emptiness because their inner life is unacknowledged and remains a mystery to them.

FAMILY STORY 1

Annette called me on the phone to schedule an IQ testing appointment for Emily. Annette explained that her son had attended Hampton, the local school for the highly gifted, many years ago. Her husband, a top investment banker, had donated large sums of money to the scholarship fund. Annette felt like they already belonged to the club.

I told Annette that entrance to Hampton School had changed since her son had been in attendance. Admission was now determined by IQ score and an interview with the new principal of the school. Nevertheless, this highly persistent mother continued to bring up her long-standing connections to the school and to her rarified world of wealth and power. I wondered if she was trying to butter me up in order to bribe me if perchance her daughter didn't score high enough on the IQ test to be admitted to Hampton. Was she thinking I would add a few extra points to the score if needed?

I met with Emily, a very sweet child who was indeed highly, frighteningly gifted. I watched the family reaction closely. Annette was delighted. She was ecstatic. Her husband tried to act surprised and humble, but I suspected that this was an act to impress me that he was a really caring father who would never push his child. Emily was just a "chip off the block." All of his children were supersmart; Emily was another notch in his belt. Though he pretended to relate to all aspects of his daughter's identity, Emily, through no fault of her own, was a narcissistic extension of her father.

Annette and her husband took their daughter's IQ score and ran straight to Hampton School. They listened to what I had to say about Emily's perfectionism as a potential problem to her overall emotional and social development, trying to convince me that they were really good parents who were seriously concerned about their daughter's emotional well-being. I didn't believe their act for a moment.

Emily got into Hampton. Annette told me that she wouldn't consider any other possibilities for schools that might help her daughter with her social shyness. She said that a parent who would look into other options was "obsessing" about the right school choice. The truth was that the Hampton School gave the parents the most visibility. Annette and her husband are most likely to tell every one of their friends about how gifted their daughter really is, while Emily's shyness and perfectionist tendencies are being ignored.

FAMILY STORY 2

Here's another perspective on the accessory parent profile involving my interactions with a young woman who worked with me in psychotherapy many years ago. I met with Annie when she was in her early 20s. She had grown up in Idaho. Her mother was an accomplished musician who was determined that all of her children achieve musical genius, because that would prove her own genius as well as help her to promote her career as the director of a symphony and music school. Unfortunately for Annie's mom, only one child showed any real musical talent. The other children had aptitude in music, but were not gifted or passionate about becoming artists. This did not stop Annie's mother, who pushed all of her children to play an instrument and to perform. Not surprisingly, the three children who were not talented musically rebelled against their mother. Annie had to leave Idaho and her mother to find her own life.

As I came to know Annie and to understand her problems with self-esteem, I realized that she was gifted verbally. However, this gift for self-expression had been ignored by her mother's focus on music. Annie spent many years of her life in California finding her "true" self. Her journey was long and heart-wrenching. Unknowingly, Annie kept sabotaging herself by falling in love with men who treated her as if she were a trophy. Her capacity to put up with inappropriate behavior and expectations from significant others—bosses and boyfriends—was truly inordinate. The legacy of her childhood had always been conditional: based on her performance or the fantasy of what she "might be." Annie had to learn to develop emotional expectations for other people in her life that mirrored her own goals and dreams. She had to learn to live for herself, not for others.

Understanding and then learning that close people in her life could love her for just being herself was at first a very torturous lesson—an almost incomprehensible idea. Many years of frequent psychotherapy provided Annie with empathy and attunement to her core true self. She began to heal from the pain of being emotionally neglected by her mother, who had required that she be a musician. Annie learned to trust herself and other people, and to fall in love with her own passions and talents. Although there was never a fairy-tale romance or a perfect job, she finally found a meaningful job and settled down with a man who loved her for who she was, not what she looked like hanging on his arm.

FAMILY STORY 3

I use the following story (based on research, not my personal involvement) as an example of parents who are narcissistically overly invested in their child. This child's life was too focused on achievement and demonstrating his abilities as a prodigy. This scenario is more common for families who are truly geographically isolated from others.

Daniel was an extremely alert and curious infant. He spoke in complete sentences by the age of 1 and taught himself to read by age of 2.

He loved numbers and was able to manipulate them in an astonishingly advanced way.

Dan's parents were very proud of his intellectual prowess and accomplishments. They decided to home school him because they were living in the high desert, isolated from other families and good schools. Dan's capacity to achieve and perform as a prodigy became the focus of family life. Normal developmental, social, and emotional issues were all ignored. Everything in life was about what Dan could do that was extraordinary. He was even a whiz kid on television.

Because of his parents' overfocus and overinvestment in his extraordinary brilliance, Daniel had been given too much support for following through on his thoughts—whatever they might be—and putting them into actions. Unfortunately, his dad had given him a gun and taught him to shoot as a child. One day, in an adolescent mood swing at the age of 14, he took his own life with his gun.

Accessory parents push their son or daughter to get the best grades at the best schools. These children win awards in every area of their lives. They are often performers and athletes. Or, unfortunately, sometimes they rebel against their parents and just stay in their rooms. Because of the emptiness of their own aspirations, they can burn out and become involved with drugs and promiscuous sexual activity. In general, children who have been pushed and used as arm candy are lost souls in search of their true selves. Gifted children who have been ignored emotionally or who have lived out their parents' dreams are inclined toward depression. Parental failure to nurture their children's inner potential and own identity creates lifelong problems when adolescence begins or when adulthood is attained.

Parents Living in Denial

While there are many parents who want to believe that their child is gifted no matter what the reality, there are also many parents who refuse to look at their children as gifted. These are the parents who choose to ignore the suggestions of pediatricians, teachers, or mentors to have their children evaluated as intellectually, musically, or artistically gifted. They decide to deny the reality of their child's potential—the opposite of accessory parents, who are overinvolved with their children's talents.

Parents in denial do not want to be bothered with the problems associated with gifted children. Half-heartedly they take their children to a psychologist, because someone else has insisted on intervention. When they are informed that their children are atypically smart, they react in a rather downtrodden manner. Parents in denial can find many reasons not to take the information about their children's gifts seriously. More often than not, the psychologist or educator who is working with them does not have the time, energy, or inclination to deal with their resistance to facing the challenge of raising a high-potential child. Let's look at some examples.

FAMILY STORY 4

Donna, an older mother, is divorced from Dave, an older and prominent computer genius and entrepreneur who has had five wives and eleven children. Zachary is the most out-of-control child in this large, blended family. Donna brings him for an evaluation because he will not behave himself at preschool. Zach is highly distractible.

After a long and extensive evaluation, the evaluator concludes that Zachary has the symptoms of a five-year-old who is gifted and bored at school. His distractibility and behavior issues would decrease if he were challenged appropriately. Donna is able to listen to this evaluation, but unfortunately, Dave rejects it. He knows what is in Zachary's best interest because, after all, he has had eleven children, has had so much success, and has made so much money. For unstated and perhaps unconscious reasons, Dave needs to deny his son's giftedness. Perhaps Dave fears his son's potential. The expert evaluator on the case is dismissed and Dave seeks the advice of yet another expert. Zachary's strengths are not addressed.

FAMILY STORY 5

Another example concerns Mr. and Mrs. Silverman, both well-educated people. Mr. Silverman is an attorney and Mrs. Silverman is a teacher. They have two children, Monica and James. Monica is a bright child who works in the top reading and math group at school. She is three years older than her brother. James is a more intense child who learned to read at the age of four. In kindergarten he is so far ahead of his class-mates in reading and mathematics that his teacher suggests that James be evaluated for a gifted school. With much reluctance, Mr. and Mrs. Silverman have him tested at a private school for highly gifted children.

James scores in the 99.9 percentile of the Stanford-Binet, and his parents are informed that 1 in 100,000 children have an IQ that is equivalent to what he has attained. James is accepted at the highly gifted school but his parents choose a public school, even though several psychologists and educators advise against it. The Silvermans want to believe that their son will get a good enough education at a regular public school. They want to give him the same education that his sister is receiving.

In first and second grade, James is bored. To make school more fun and to get attention, he is the class clown. He hides under the tables and distracts other children whenever he can get away with it. By third grade he is hanging out with the "bad" kids at school. By sixth grade, James is a troublemaker who is labeled as a delinquent. In desperation Mr. and Mrs. Silverman have to send their son to a school out of state for teenagers with behavioral problems.

Highly religious families often fall into denial about the needs of their smart children, because they value a spiritual religious education over the child's unique learning strengths and chal-lenges. I have seen many instances where Jewish, Catholic, or Protestant beliefs and the church or temple community took precedence over the gifted child's special learning needs. This is an unfortunate situation because children with extreme intel-lectual and creative capacities need to be challenged and understood by their teachers. While I believe that religious schools can provide for children with special learning challenges, on most occasions the school administrator did not take seriously the problems and challenges of the gifted. And, in turn, maybe parents who choose religious schools believe in a more traditional approach to education, which may lack the creativity a gifted child needs to thrive at school.

Parents Who Work with the Whole Gifted Child

Concerned parents give a lot of thought to their children's education and the developmental and emotional issues that contribute to a healthy and well-adjusted child. They learn how to evaluate their son's or daughter's progress, and work toward developing realistic expectations, not expectations that pressure their children. When they encounter a problem they look for a solution. They have a plan of action regarding their child's education. These types of parents think seriously about socialization issues that their son or daughter may have because of their giftedness.

My professional experiences have mostly been with parents who have deep concerns about the overall development and education of their gifted children. I have a great deal of empathy for parents who face the reality that they have a child with "over the top" potential. Within this context, I have come to understand that shock, and then disbelief, is a normal reaction to being told that you have a highly gifted child, even if you know in your heart that your child is "quirky" for this very reason. The fear that you will not be able to live up to a demanding parenting role is also behind this reaction. At the same time, I think parents are relieved to know that someone knows their "secret" because it reduces the burden of being alone with your most intimate and intense thoughts. Parents who react strongly are the most realistic, as they are best able to deal with and develop their gifted child's potential.

Struggling to Understand

To illustrate my point about how a concerned parent can react, I include the previously mentioned actress Linda's thoughts, which she presented at the California Gifted Association Conference in 2004.

"Tested? What do you mean, 'tested'? Tested for what? IQ? She's not even five. Aren't I curious? No, I'm not curious. I don't want to know. I don't need to know. Do I? I mean, do I really need to know? But, you think she's what? How can you tell?— All she's been doing is coloring. You can tell by that? Gifted? Oh, you mean artistic. Academically gifted? No, no, she's not gifted; she's normal.

"The words came tumbling out of my mouth, so many non-sequiturs. I wished I wasn't a part of this equation, just a fly on the wall. I was trying to keep my growing curiosity at bay because I needed to resist succumbing to this highly educated, charismatic individual who was preying on my maternal hopes and insecurities. Qualities, I assured myself, which were inherent in first-time mothers.

"Why did I feel so compelled to protect my daughter's normalcy? What was 'normal' anyway?

"Bottom line: I was afraid. Afraid to have her tested. There, I said it. Afraid she wouldn't pass. Can you not pass an IQ test? If she didn't pass, does that mean she had failed? Was it black, white, or could she be gray?

"I didn't want to subject my precious child to some mind-probing examination. Didn't want to leave her for any length of time, while she was queried ad nauseam, and made to perform tasks like a trained seal. I had all these convoluted ideas about what this test involved, ideas that drove my anxieties to new levels.

"I had taken no commensurate exam from which to draw conclusions. Only the IOWA test I was required to take when I was a young girl. The ones with all the little dots you colored in with the requisite 'number 2 pencil.' The myriad dots I always filled in randomly, out of sheer boredom.

"To test or not to test, that is the question. Succumb, I finally did. You colossally persuasive, exquisitely brilliant doctor, may I present my daughter, the guinea pig?

"Barnes and Noble, there I went; I had to get books. When in doubt, read a book. I had to understand what 'gifted' meant. After all, it was just past Christmas, I had been gifted, I had gifted others and now I must have a gifted child? Wherein lay the difference?

"Shocking, an absolutely shocking void of material on gifted children. One book, only one book! I devoured it and then reined myself in: she was still being tested, over-zealous me. At least I was the proud possessor of earth-shattering knowledge: 160 was a 'genius' IQ! I had lived all these years believing an IQ of 140 was 'genius.' What a waste, all those years, utterly uninformed.

"She passed, my beautiful, challenging, independent child, she the veracious digester of any and all information, had passed. Okay, so she wasn't destined to be gray. I still didn't want a number. Didn't need to hear a number. Pass or fail, true or false, always the best options.

"Suddenly, I had answers to all of my daughter's behavioral idiosyncrasies. She did this because she was highly gifted; she did that because she was highly gifted. Was there anything she did *not* do, because she was highly gifted?

"I began to refer to this syndrome by its initials: H.G. My daughter is affected with H.G.-ness.

"Who could I talk to about this? Doctor, you seemed thrilled. I caught the 'I told you so' glint in your perceptive eyes. Well, 'un-gift' her!

"I didn't need this. It had taken months to get rid of her perpetual throat clearing. I even had the pediatrician take a look and I had not even *begun* to address the new blinking issue.

"I'll call the husband and tell him the news, relate this impressive score. Yes, by now I knew the number, silly little number.

"Doctor, you promised not to tell me. Just slipped out, huh?

"Back to the husband; great, he said it was great. Great? What was great about it? She was forever labeled, a card-carrying member of what?

"I needed to tell someone! Anyone! No, not you, doctor, with those two Ph.D.s of yours. I needed a real person. Someone who had kids, little kids like mine, not big grown-up ones that were already baked to perfection.

"Oh yeah, but *please* keep the H.G. books coming. Maybe Freud, Piaget, or Jung, these erudite entities, might have some answers for me.

"Then it dawned on me, maybe there had been an error. Maybe the test had malfunctioned. Spit out an erroneous score. Maybe my ever-so-manipulative offspring had found a method to charm her way into the 99th percentile. Maybe they gave extra points for being cute."

Linda's thoughts cleverly dramatize her struggle to understand what it means to have a highly gifted child. Linda's anxiety about the process of identification of giftedness and her concern that her child is not normal is quite common. As well, her need to talk openly about her own feelings and concerns that raising a gifted child will be a difficult task is very adaptive.

Doubting Your Own Perception

Janice the attorney—having grown up in Ivy League schools rather than in European private schools and on a sound stage like Linda— looks at the problem of having a highly gifted child from a different perspective. Janice writes:

"To tell the truth, I expected my children to be very smart. Why not? I was, and so was my mother, and so were their fathers (two children, two genetic fathers), and I read enough to know the importance of heredity. Also, to tell the truth, it was important to me that my children be smart. Not geniuses, but smart. This wasn't an accessory-child thing. Being smart was what had saved me from a very difficult childhood. In my mind, being smart and being able to survive were much the same thing.

"My first child did indeed seem very smart in his first four years (very smart and very serious and very verbal). But he did not seem like an obvious genius, and in the East Coast intellectual center where I lived at the time, he did not seem particularly unusual—there were at least two other children with equivalent verbal skills in his university-based preschool. So, I decided my first-born was merely bright. This seemed to be confirmed when he resisted reading and the principal of the local school recommended we hold him back a year. Even then, starting first grade at age seven, he needed the help of a reading specialist into mid-year.

"So in my mind, my oldest was pegged merely 'bright.' He stayed that way even when, just a year later in second grade, we received the results of a state reading test that told us he was now reading at high-school level. It didn't help when we moved to California and the local public school advised us, on the basis of a group-administered test, that he was 'gifted' but not 'highly gifted.'

"Then he started having trouble at the same public school—real trouble. He was zoning out in class, reading under the desk, daydreaming. We took him to a psychologist for testing. She told us he was indeed bright. Very, very bright. Very, very, very, bright. The problem wasn't our son. It was the school.

"Since then, everything has been much easier. I no longer doubt the test scores that come back, from both the testing firms and the Johns Hopkins programs. Our oldest is 'severely gifted'—he will never be 'normal,' nor should we want him to be. Understanding this has made it much easier for us to get along with him and for him to get along with us (although a good portion of his now-private school teachers still don't quite get it). And we have no doubts at all about our second son. We don't need any more tests to convince us he, too, is 'severely gifted.'

"Why did it take us a while to get comfortable with this reality? Three reasons, I think.

"First, knowing how psychologically important it was to me that my children be smart, I was inclined to doubt my own perceptions and dismiss them as wishful thinking.

"Second, when the perfectionism often associated with highly gifted children interfered with my oldest child's initial foray into reading, this seemed to confirm the less-than-genius hypothesis.

"Third, living only among upper-class professionals (many of them university professors) had given me a very distorted view of what was 'normal' child development. Thank goodness we now have a more accurate view. Sure, there may be many highly gifted kids out there in the world. But not enough to make it easy for either the kids or their parents. We can't fix that reality, but recognizing it allows us to avoid at least some bumps in the road."

What is important to underline is the confusion that the label of giftedness brings to a household. Janice's impression that perceptions of her child's giftedness were merely wishful thinking is common. Smart parents want smart children. And they can and do get confused about their own feelings and perceptions about their children's gifts.

Challenges Down the Road

Cynthia, an experienced teacher and mother, writes candidly about the long-range problems she foresees with her son.

"How does it feel being the mom of a gifted child? It has changed over the years. At first, when he was very young, I think it was just amazement. Being an elementary school teacher, I knew what was normal developmentally. And Jorge was not normal. He started talking early, knew his numbers and letters and was reading simple words. Two-year-olds do not normally teach themselves how to write on a Magna-Doodle! But along with my amazement came a little fear . . . oh my God! What are we going to do with him when he gets to school?

"Now that he is six and in school, and moving faster than even I expected, it's a little daunting. Going through this process of getting him tested is both a relief (how we'll know exactly what we're dealing with—how gifted he really is) and over-whelming (now we're finding out exactly what we're dealing with and how gifted he is!). Now there is this extra huge re-sponsibility of making sure that we continue to meet his ex-traordinary needs. Being a teacher is helpful, in a way. But even I have limitations. And being a Mom is completely different than being someone's teacher. Besides dealing with his insatiable appetite to learn new things, I also have to deal with the moods, the sensitivity, the impatience, the demands. He is a needy kid. And I don't send him home to someone else at 2:30. He comes home to me.

"It's not all bad. These are just some of the frustrations I've experienced. But I know I am blessed. I know I have a special, special, child. As much frustration as he brings me, he brings even more joy. We can't imagine our lives without him. And all we really want is for him to be happy. I hope we can continue to make sure he is getting what he needs to be able to live a pro-ductive, happy life. We have many years to go, so I guess we just have to be patient with ourselves and continue to learn how to do the best we can."

What strikes me in Cynthia's thoughts is her understanding that she learned something about giftedness by working as a teacher. She is able to see her child's gifts and honestly talk about how she sees her challenges as a parent. She rightly feels a huge responsibility to meet his needs both emotionally and intellectually.

Calmly Expecting the News

George, a surgeon who attended my parenting group, adds a dif-ferent insight into how parents react to the news that their child is gifted. George says:

"I am a calm person. I deal with life and death situations on a regular basis with my own patients. So when you discussed my son's IQ, I felt enlightened by the information. It was interesting to find out where Jacob stood in relationship to other children. I never really thought about how smart my son would be. But I also expected him to be smart because all of my family members are very smart and very accomplished. I think it would be stressful *not* to have a gifted child. I am used to working with other doctors who are very bright and quick to get information. It would be awkward if my son was just average.

"When Jacob was young a friend told me he thought my kid was gifted. In my generation we never heard about these distinctions in IQ. I think it is just a different vocabulary. When I was growing up they called me really smart."

George Cramer's reaction may seem understated compared to other reactions I have heard in my groups or working with clients. Knowing Dr. Cramer helps me to fill in the blanks for you. George is very concerned about being the best parent he can possibly be to Jacob. Dr. and Mrs. Cramer have focused on giving Jacob a warm and nurturing home and they have sent him to a private school that they believe will enhance his individual learning strengths and style.

George's insight that giftedness is a new way to talk about an old phenomena—the smart child—is very accurate. Prior to the 1970s the label of giftedness was not widespread. Smart children were thought to be nerds or eggheads, no matter what. The literature on the smart child did not take into account that bright children have different needs when it comes to their social and emotional development. The gifted label, a revision of the smart child, takes the whole child into consideration.

Understanding the Wide Variability

Ellen, a very devoted mother, film producer, and long-time member of my parenting group, writes about how difficult it has been to accept the idiosyncrasies of her gifted son. Ellen has never been in denial, but has had reservations about the label of gifted child.

Her questioning fear—"Are you telling me the truth?"—is one that I am quite familiar with from working with other parents.

> "With our first child, my husband and I didn't have any basis of comparison to know if our son was average or gifted. We sometimes wondered when he spoke sentences before his buddies at daycare had uttered 'bye-bye' or when he began doing multiplication in kindergarten if he was different than other kids. I assumed all parents thought their kids were gifted until I read an article that said that if you suspect that your child is gifted, there's a good chance he is.
>
> "In kindergarten and first grade, teachers said that he 'thought differently' or reminded them of some other gifted child they knew, but nobody came out and said he was 'gifted.' Actually, he didn't do that well in school: he often called out, seemed distracted, and wasn't do anything extraordinary like writing symphonies or memorizing all the president's names like the kids on TV do.
>
> "In second grade, his teacher told us that he was 'developmentally lagging' and lacked concentration skills. She didn't quite think he had ADD but that he was just immature. He would 'fidget' and 'drop his pencil.' The biggest problem was that our son, who was doing algebra at home, couldn't seem to complete a simple math test of 20 addition problems. Finally, a teacher was telling us the truth . . . he needed to mature and finish his work. He was just normal and he needed a tougher hand.
>
> "A few weeks later, the same teacher called me frantically to her room to tell me that she had just returned from a conference on gifted children. She showed me a page of notes on the characteristics of gifted children, and beside all of them she had written my son's name. She was sure she had been mistaken and that his distracted behavior was a sign of his giftedness. She requested testing and, sure enough, the school psychologist found his achievement, other than math, only slightly above normal, but his intelligence tests showed him to be highly gifted.
>
> "Disbelieving that the public school psychologist knew anything, we consulted a psychologist, who proclaimed that she was positive just from speaking with him that he was gifted. We

then had a WISC III test administered that scored him even higher. Our response was that the psychologist had made a mistake. How could he be highly gifted; he didn't do anything spectacular. He was just a normal kid who loved baseball and Game Boy. He didn't sit around reading all day, play the violin, or come up with scientific theories.

"Gradually and reluctantly, we accepted that his giftedness presented itself in a higher cognition, in a way of solving problems outside the norm. He began to complain that school was repetitive and that as soon as a subject got interesting, the teacher changed the subject. We started to see that he was uttering the very common problem of highly gifted children who require less repetition and greater immersion. His math ability kept growing, but he wasn't just solving problems—he was moving numbers around his head and understanding the global concept of numbers. He was writing interesting sentences about boring topics and begging to be part of academic summer programs.

His *hyperness* and oversensitive behavior began to make sense. His love of long evening talks when he should be sleeping and his hatred of repeating math problems over and over had an explanation. His inability to write as fast as he could think and his frustration with other children who refused to follow the rules of a game made sense. His lack of organization with some things and his intense focus on the organization of things that interested him fell into place. He was actually a typical gifted child, but because he wasn't a prodigy it was difficult for us to accept. He just seemed so normal on so many levels.

"We still doubt his test scores when he blows an achievement test or doesn't care about something that we think should interest him. Sometimes we are positive that he's brilliant while other times we think it's all been a mistake. A high-achieving kid would be much easier to understand and raise; however, our gifted child (or is he?) makes life so much more interesting."

Later in this book I will write about common learning problems of gifted children, which in most instances are related to their perfectionist nature. I think that Ellen describes with very specific details how confusing it can be to understand the highs and lows of the gifted child. Her story points out the wide variability within the gifted category.

Dealing with Developmental Issues

Angela talks about how her son's developmental issues had more of an impact on her than the understanding that he was gifted.

"When I learned my son is gifted, I had mixed emotions. Part of me felt relieved. At a very young age he had been diagnosed with a mild case of Asperger's Syndrome. From the minute I heard those words I focused on helping him with his social skills. And, in that respect, helping him 'catch up' with his peers.

"It was nice to validate his intellectual strength, which I knew would help him work through some of his areas of challenge. On the other hand, I now had the responsibility to see to it that his hungry little mind would be adequately nourished in his educational (and noneducational) environments. I had a new and better framework in my mind of the types of things I had to consider when thinking about his schools, summer programs, after-school activities, music, etc. When I say framework, I mean more than just intellectual capability, but all of the strengths, challenges, interests, disinterests, feelings, beliefs, and values that come together in the world of my precious child.

"High intelligence was another factor in a world of many factors. And his brightness had been pointed out to me before, but I just wasn't sure about what level he was on. I had listened to enough parents bragging about gifted kids that I knew I was not going to tell anyone outside of my family and the professionals (mainly teachers) working with him. I later found it interesting and insightful to talk with other parents of gifted children, knowing that this personal information was safe with that group."

The parents who share their thoughts illustrate my point about concerned parents' intense reactions when they are told that their child is gifted. Concerned parents who believe that their child is gifted take the situation seriously. They try to address their "whole child" instead of focusing on aspects of their child that they are comfortable with.

In contrast, accessory parents are absolutely delighted that they have a little genius. It makes them look even smarter. Those parents who are living in denial try to ignore the messenger who tells them that their child has special learning issues. Parents in denial cannot focus on their child's gifts because they are overwhelmed by their own problems. Accessory parents and deniers don't want to look at the whole challenge of raising a gifted child. Rather, they look at *aspects* of their child; they have a distorted perspective. And the parents' misperception of their own children make the gifted child vulnerable to depression, burnout, and poor self-esteem.

Being a Concerned Parent

Simple as it may sound, you need to listen to and observe your child. Then you need to react to your inner thoughts and understandings about your child. Your job is to always react when your child is communicating with you. A parent's reactions are so telling, important, and truthful. You need to learn to trust yourself and your instincts about your child. Your parenting will go forward more easily because your children will be seen and valued for who they are, as opposed to children whose parents hold unrealistic expectations regarding who they should be or hopes regarding who they might become.

The "best way" or the "right way" to deal with a gifted child is to gradually acknowledge, and come to accept, that you are facing a challenge. By a country mile, your child will not be the easiest kid on the block to raise because of his or her energy, curiosity, intelligence, and sensitivity. Whatever glory you may receive from others because of their talents or genius will not come the easy way. You will have to spend time and thought developing their talents. Parenting a gifted child is truly a challenge.

I suggest that first you look inside yourself for guidance. Ask yourself:

1. When did I first start to think that my child was gifted?
2. Am I comfortable having a gifted child? If yes, why? Or why not?
3. What is special about my child?
4. What tasks does my child struggle to complete?
5. Is my child like me, my husband, his parents, or my parents?
6. Where can I learn about raising a gifted child?
7. Who can guide me in raising my child?
8. Where can I find other parents with similar parenting problems?
9. Are there schools in my community that understand the special needs of gifted children?

How to Be a "Good Enough" Parent to Your Gifted Child

Because there is no agreed-upon definition of giftedness, under-standing the needs of particularly talented children can be prob-lematic. Giftedness means different things to different people. To make this situation even more complicated, most educators have strong negative reactions to claims of giftedness by parents. If I close my eyes, I can imagine the following conversation between parent and teacher. This conversation is my nightmare rerun of a troubling movie that I have seen far too many times. The parent, looking in-nocently and anxiously, is almost begging for help: "I think my child is gifted." The teacher, with an apprehensive, fearful look, responds in a cold and negative tone: "What do you mean when you say your child is gifted? How do you know? Were there standardized tests used for the evaluation? I want to see them."

Instantly, the parent is put on the spot. The parent was already stressed out because of her concern about her gifted child, and now the teacher has become an adversary instead of an ally. And, most likely, the teacher is stressed because she or he feels pressured by the stereotype of a gifted child's parent.

I myself wonder who should take care of the gifted child's special needs. According to the law, the local public school is responsible for meeting each and every child's individual needs. From my 30 years of experience, I know that public or private schools will not provide for the gifted child based on one simple request. Rather, parents have to at least "insist" that their children be evaluated, and they have to face the scorn and disbelief of educators.

As a concerned parent, hopefully you will figure out how to deal with or get what you want from your child's school by talking to other parents and educators, and by doing research on the Internet, in the bookstore, or at the library. Actually, I believe that the doubletalk and confusion about standards and measurements that you hear from teachers and administrators is just a diversionary strategy to wipe out the problem of the gifted child entirely. From the administrative point of view, the gifted child requires too much undivided attention. Unfortunately, it is common for educators to band together and ignore the gifted child. Fortunately, gifted children usually have gifted parents who will see through this disinterest— parents who do not accept obliviousness and doubletalk. And some parents are successful in getting the support they need from schools. You want to put yourself in this group.

Giftedness definitely has genetic components, but genetics alone will not ensure that giftedness manifests itself. Giftedness or talent will grow in the right environment, lay dormant in a nonsupportive environment, and be destroyed in a hostile milieu. Giftedness is like a flower that blooms from season to season, dependent on the environment that nurtures and protects it. The better suited the environment for the particular talent, the more likely it is to flourish—and sadly, giftedness or talent can be squandered. There is something truly distasteful about wasting the richness of young minds and souls that our culture is seemingly indifferent to.

Variations in Giftedness

We know that giftedness exists because we can see it in the world around us. The musical genius of Mozart, the paintings of Georgia O'Keefe, the poetry of James Joyce, the brilliance of a performance by Tom Hanks, the miracles of the scientists who discover cures for cancer, the beauty and strength of a Frank Gehry building, the courage and skills of men like John Glenn, and so on—these contributions to society are immeasurable, whether or not these individuals' IQs were measured by a standardized test.

There are extreme variations in giftedness. Not all gifted children will score high on the Stanford-Binet or Wechsler Scale because not all gifted children are alike. Some gifted children are interested in rocket science, some are interested in dissecting frogs and fetal pigs, some want to read Latin, others are redesigning the family home, some compose music or want to perform at Carnegie Hall, and so on.

What is similar among these variations is that all of these gifted children have an intense passion to understand and master whatever is making them curious. They are extremely quick to learn and do not give up until they fully understand what they are curious about. They are persistent about needing to know and will pursue their passion over their lifetime.

Let's look at snapshots of six different young gifted children as they illustrate the potential variations in gifted children.

The Designer

Jacob and his parents, Dr. and Mrs. Cramer, met with me to have their son evaluated for a private gifted school. Dr. and Mrs.

Cramer are very devoted parents to their only son. They put a great deal of thought into the selection of Jacob's preschool and elementary school, with very good results. Jacob is a happy child who loves his friends, school, athletics, music, and drawing. On meeting with Jacob, you can pick up on his sweet and shy nature. Jacob's IQ is in the highly gifted range. In fact, it's off the charts when it comes to his greatest strength—his ability to understand abstract design.

Jacob is starting first grade. He began to read at the end of kindergarten. And then he proceeded to read at an eighth-grade level within five months. Jacob has problems with his perfectionism. He had to be able to read perfectly before he thought he wanted to read at all.

The Collector

Ryan, age six, is the oldest son of two young up-and-coming attorneys. Ryan is an intense and verbal child who spoke like a little adult by the age of two. He is outgoing and never misses the opportunity for fun or trouble.

Ryan is a collector of objects from coins to action figures, from baseball cards and books to records. His room sometimes looks like a vintage warehouse or an extremely cluttered place in need of a dumpster or a garage sale. Ryan won't permit the loss of a single collectable. His parents aren't sure what all this "stuff" means to Ryan so they let him keep his collections. Ryan has lots of friends who visit his collection room. He is a happy child and curious about everything that he sees and everyone he meets.

Because of his energy and quickness and his ability to talk about his ideas in the first grade, Ryan is tested by the school psychologist for the gifted program, using a Stanford-Binet IQ test. Ryan makes the cut and is placed in the gifted program because of his strong verbal abilities, mathematical reasoning, and good judgment. His parents are proud of him. They encourage him to follow his heart.

The Mathematician

Christina is the youngest daughter of Drs. Nancy and Mark Monroe, who are college professors. Christina is a shy child who is happy with just a few select friends. Christina loves her doll collection, but she is also very interested in cars and computers. She can play alone in her room for hours on end. Her parents often take Christina to science museums, as she loves this type of stimulation.

Christina attends a developmental preschool at the university where her parents are teachers. When she starts kindergarten she is reading. But her strength and passion is in mathematics. Christina can do third-grade math in kindergarten.

Christina is placed in the gifted class, which is very accelerated. Christina has several friends in the gifted class, but she remains shy on the playground. She is a follower in social situations, but academically she is the leader of the pack. Christina competes for the Math Club and brings her school honors.

The Globally Gifted

Allison is the oldest adopted daughter of Natalie and David Chang, who are prominent art dealers. Allison is a natural athlete and a nonstop talker. As a baby, Allison loved to be with other children. Natalie participated with Allison in as many Mommy and Me classes as she could find to feed Allison's socialization needs. The other mothers called Allison the "genius child" because she was so advanced. By 18 months, Allison was able to sing and dance the alphabet song by herself.

As a five-year-old, Allison has at least five best friends. She is invited to every birthday party. She is an accomplished gymnast. Allison attended a Montessori preschool, where she could work at her own pace. Now in kindergarten, Allison is capable of doing third-grade work in reading and math. She is evaluated for a private school and the psychologist tells her mother that she is talented in so many areas that she should be given the label of "globally gifted."

The Psychologist

Ben Nilsson is the oldest child of two prominent lawyers. Ben is a very sensitive child who blames himself when something goes wrong. He is placed in a Montessori preschool, where he does very well because the focus is on individual development.

In kindergarten, Ben attends an excellent public school, but he has some difficulty with this transition. He is easily bored with more typical children and less challenging work. Ben can be disorganized about his school work, and he has a hard time learning to read. School evaluations suggest that he is a gifted child and very much a perfectionist.

Ben learns to read in second grade, and by third grade he can read at a college level. He is a compassionate and introspective child who likes to have a few close friends. Ben is very insightful and looks at other people's way of doing things—their motivations. His mother believes that he will be a psychologist when he grows up. Both of his parents are pleased about his intellectual curiosity and his insight into other people, although they are not always sure how to develop this aspect of his inner life. After a great deal of consideration, they make sure that the school he attends is academically rigorous and has a great deal of enrichment and creative activities.

The Artist

Rachel is the only daughter of older parents who are both medical doctors. Rachel is a difficult baby, and her mother suspects that she may have a behavioral disorder. Rachel is diagnosed with a mild case of Asperger's Syndrome, which is on the autistic spectrum. The developmental pediatrician prescribes intensive behavioral therapy for her. Rachel receives a comprehensive behavioral intervention, which works on helping her socialization experiences.

By age five, Rachel is able to attend a regular kindergarten. She quickly learns to read, and by second grade she can read and do math that is two to three grades above her age level. Rachel loves to draw, and her pictures show her talent. Rachel has a sensitive and shy personality, and her family believes that drawing is her way of expressing herself. Rachel is also highly verbal and can explain her thoughts and feelings in great detail. Not unexpectedly, Rachel is shy in social situations.

Commonalities Between Gifted Children

All of these children display characteristics of giftedness—quickness to learn, a rage to master, an ability to work at an advanced level at certain tasks, persistence to understand a task and complete it, and an ability to translate their inner passions or an understanding of life to the world. These children also differ in the types of giftedness they possess.

- Ryan is academically advanced, introspective, social, and psychologically minded.
- Rachel is extremely sensitive and perceptive, but her talent is artistic.
- Christina is mathematically inclined.
- Jacob, who is gifted verbally and mathematically, is able to work two years above grade level and has a visual ability that will allow him to soar in engineering or architecture.
- Allison is extremely socially sophisticated, talented as a gymnast, and is a star student in her gifted classroom.
- Ben may be the next Sigmund Freud.

What is critical for you to understand is that gifted children are very insistent about mastery, and this drive will lead to perfectionism and heightened sensitivity to others. Learning to deal with perfectionism is the next concept that you must understand as you struggle to raise your gifted child.

Do Not Try to Be the Perfect Parent to Your Gifted Child

Immediately give up any impulse or fantasy that you can raise your gifted child perfectly. *Good enough* is really enough. These energy-draining children are hard to raise as it is. Making mistakes is normal. Not knowing the best course of action to take is completely understandable. There are no road maps. There is no owner's manual. There is a very limited selection of developmental books you can read that will give you the answers to all your questions on how to deal with your little genius. Many of these sources on gifted children can be misleading. And some of the advice and answers won't apply to your child. Or, you might find that there are conflicting or confusing opinions on raising very smart children.

Tony, a mother in my parenting group since we began several years ago, writes the following poignant and humorous advice to a newly informed mother of a gifted child:

1. Forget everything you thought you knew about raising children.

2. Forget everything you thought you knew about budgeting.

3. Collect all your books about parenting, discipline & such, make a ditch, squirt a little kerosene and light. You might do this with your new friends at a support group and make it a "moment." Make a ring around the bonfire and sing:

   Amazing grace,
   How sweet the thought.

Please save this mom you see.
Please reimburse
These books I bought.
They don't apply to me.

Not only is it unrealistic and a waste of time to try to be a perfect parent to an energy-draining gifted child but, psychologically speaking, your own perfectionist tendencies will encourage your child to be even more intense and fearful. For example, many parents become frantic about the right foods, clothes, school, toys, and so on. Your children pick up on your concerns and learn to worry as well.

Perfectionism is a trait that needs to be tamed and put in a semblance of control in both you and your child. If your child sees that you are attempting to be perfect, he or she will try to learn from your strategies. Often, gifted children will figure out what you are trying to accomplish in terms of a child-rearing plan. When they can't succeed in pleasing you, they may feel overwhelmed and defeated. They may believe that they have disappointed you. This is, to say the least, the worst way to develop self-esteem in a child. As they say, the road to hell is paved with good intentions.

Because they are very perceptive and insightful, gifted children will pick up on your unspoken expectations. I recall the unfortunate example of Anita, who couldn't make up her mind about what she expected of her highly gifted son, Jon. On the one hand, Anita was casual, open-minded, and child-centered. For example, it was okay with her if Jon decided on his own about which friends and play dates he wanted. On the other hand, she could be extremely strict about doing school work: "Do your homework perfectly." There was a contradiction in messages that her gifted son could feel, if not comprehend. Since his mother changed her mind so often, Jon was confused and fearful about what was going to happen next. Reading his mother's moods and doing what she expected became a full-time preoccupation. Jon began to fear the worst—that he could do nothing right. His self-esteem and confidence vanished, and he became afraid to go to school.

This is an extreme example used to point out that gifted children are sensitive to their parents' expectations, moods, and values. Very bright children know what you are saying as well as the unstated subtext. And they most likely recognize what you are *not* saying. So when gifted children see perfectionism as an overriding family value, they will intensify their own internal quest to do their own activities and play perfectly. Or the opposite may occur. A gifted child will give up entirely if they imagine that certain tasks with high parental expectations are just too hard to accomplish.

How to Keep Perfectionist Tendencies in Check

Giving up on your own perfectionist strivings is critical to becoming a good-enough parent. You need to be aware of what your actions are telling your children. Let's look at three different examples. These three families are presented to illustrate my point that family expectations, whether directly stated or unstated, are transmitted to your child.

First, we'll look at a family who has their own perfectionism under control. They are a child-centered family. And yet, they have not given up the need for order and structure in their family life.

A CHILD-CENTERED FAMILY

Beatrice and Daniel are young parents. They are intelligent and high-achieving professionals who want the best of everything for Sara, their first child. They are determined not to make the same mistakes as their unavailable parents. They believe that family life is crucial to Sara's development.

Bea works part time, and still she has taken time off from her work to observe the preschools in her neighborhood. She is looking for a developmentally focused school that is concerned with the whole child. While she and her husband believe that reading, writing, and math are crucial to a proper education, they also believe that three years old is way too early to begin with academic pressure. However, they want some structure at their daughter's school and a variety of activities.

Bea and Dan select a Montessori school because of its individualized approach to learning. Bea knows that Sara is good at focusing on certain cognitive tasks, but has difficulty following simple rules. Bea is highly creative and likes to make up her own rules. Since Sara is an only child, Bea likes the heavy emphasis on socialization at the Montessori school. Dan agrees with his wife; he believes Sara will benefit from learning to play cooperatively with other children. Playing cooperatively is sometimes a problem for Sara, who is used to playing on her own, without other children.

Sara is a creative child who is very active and enjoys playing with her dolls, books, and arts and crafts projects. Bea and Dan take Sara to the park every day, where she has lots of children she can chum around with in the sand or on the grass, if she feels so inclined. Sara behaves herself at mealtime, but does not like to clean up or go to bed on time. If her dad had the time and patience, she would have him reading to her until dawn.

Bea and Dan have made some rules for Sara that they are firm that she follow. Bedtime is at 8:00. Clean-up is always necessary. Television is limited to one hour a day. While these rules are followed, Bea and Dan have child-friendly expectations. Clean-up does not have unrealistic expectations of total order, but a realistic child order. Bedtime can vary for special occasions, which are decided in advance. Certain time extensions for television or movies are made if there is something worth watching.

The family home is neat and clean, but not fastidious. Bea's mother is an interior designer and she has purchased some beautiful furniture for Ben and Dan's living room. Dan's parents are art dealers and they have given the couple some beautiful and interesting art, which is placed in certain adult areas of their home. Sara has been told and understands what she can and cannot play with. The rest of the house is more child-centered and relaxed. Sara understands and easily adheres to the general house rules about "children spaces" and "adult spaces."

The family time that Bea and Dan and Sara spend together is important to all of them. They guard this time preciously because it develops a strong family bond. Family time also helps Bea and Dan understand what is going on in Sara's life. As a family they travel to visit grandparents and to explore cities and national parks. Family life has been structured with realistic child expectations in mind.

Bea and Dan have noticed that Sara has to do everything perfectly. Sara often cries when she can't master a task. Both parents talk with their daughter about how everyone makes mistakes. Bea and Dan talk with Sara about specific experiences where they have made mistakes. They reassure her that she does not have to master tasks that are too hard for a young child. Besides reassuring Sara that she is a competent child, they also distract Sara when she gets overly involved in trying to accomplish a task perfectly.

Now let's look at an example of a family who has opposite values and parenting strategies.

A PERFECTLY ORDERED FAMILY—LINDA, MIKE, AND JASON

Linda and Mike are professionals in their early thirties. They own a beautiful house and have a full-time housekeeper. They have done enough financial planning for Linda to be able to stay home when she has her children. They look forward to their first child. During her pregnancy, Linda decorates the "perfect" nursery for her son. As excited and positively expectant as they can be, Linda and Mike are not prepared for the demands of parenthood. Jason is a high-strung baby. Linda's mother is of no help because she cannot deal with the chaos that a baby brings to a well-kept house. Linda is exhausted all of the time and hires a nanny to help her because Mike is always at work.

Jason is a very active child who is full of energy and has an enormous curiosity. Linda is a very nervous mother who does not know what to expect from her child. She reads all the latest baby books and joins a parenting group to educate herself and gain support from other parents. Helpful advice goes into one ear and out the other. Her overriding concern remains keeping her house clean for Mike and her mother. Jason is relegated to a small corner of the house, which is next to the housekeeper, called the play room. Jason gets in trouble when he ventures out of his part of the house.

Jason is a very smart and very sensitive child. He senses that he is not totally welcome in his family. In anger and frustration, Jason is always trying to make a mess in a room where he does not belong. There is a great deal of tension in the family because of the unstated expectation that life will proceed as it did before Jason was born.

When Jason is two, Linda finally takes the advice of a friend who has young children and calls a child development specialist, Dr. L., who immediately picks up on the rigidity of the household. She suggests that Jacob's anger is related to the lack of attention he receives from his father and the overconcern for adult order in the house. Dr. L. helps Linda make her house more child-centered by developing rules that Jason can follow with success. Mike spends more time with his son on the weekend. Jason is given more open space in his home. Understandably and predictably, Jason's behavioral problems are reduced.

Jason attends a very academically structured preschool, which begins to teach four-year-olds prereading skills. Both Linda and Michael want their son to start achieving in academics as early in life as possible. There is stated and unstated pressure for Jason to master all of the tasks that are presented to him, from school to sports to music.

At school, Jason is a high-strung and moody child. His teachers describe him as anxious. Mike and Linda are unaware of how they contribute to their son's emotional problems. They have almost no insight into how gifted their son really is. They do not understand how to deal with his perfectionism. They have no interest in attending to his non-traditional learning style and needs.

Let's look at another example of "over" involved parents, which illustrates how parents can be so perfectly tuned into their child that they create an emotional tyrant who has difficulties getting along with others.

AN OVERLY CHILD-FOCUSED FAMILY—GAIL, MATT, AND SUSAN

Jane and Matt are professionals who met and married in their mid-thirties. Both bring a great deal of career experience to the marriage, but very little in the way of relationship experiences. Both are very independent and not particularly interested in a traditional family life. Jane becomes pregnant after three months of marriage. When their daughter, Susan, is born, Jane and Matt buy a house in a reasonably nice neighborhood. Susan becomes the total focus of the family home. Susan has her own bedroom. And yet, her extra crib is placed in the dining room. Actually, the whole house looks like it was designed for Susan. Jane gives up her consulting business to care for Susan full time. Matt goes to work all day, and when he comes home he devotes all of his evening hours to Susan. Jane and Matt seem to have no life together except for their concern for Susan.

Susan is a difficult and fussy baby who gets way too much attention for every move she makes. Every moment of Susan's life is an issue for her parents. For example, Susan is not allowed to go outside until she is nine months old because her parents worry that she will catch a cold. Fortunately, Jane reads many parenting books and she realizes that Susan needs to be with other children for her social development.

Finally, Jane takes Susan to the park and to other activities for toddlers. Susan is enrolled in the best preschool that her parents can find, which feeds into an elementary school. Jane does not like attending parenting meetings or support groups because she believes she is smarter than the other mothers. Matt is shy and prefers not to socialize with other parents.

Nothing is too much for this child. By the time Susan is five, the family room has a gymnasium floor with a ballet bar so that Susan can study ballet privately. The backyard contains outdoor equipment worthy of a preschool. Collections of Susan's toys, books, movies, and musical instruments fill the house. Susan's drawings from the age of two are framed and cover the walls of the upstairs and downstairs of the family home.

Susan expects everything to be done to suit her needs. Although she likes school, she has difficulties making friends because she is so used to being the center of attention. Consequently, she is not very advanced at playing or sharing.

Jane micro-manages Susan, always making sure that the teachers are not being too hard on her child or that the coaches of the sports teams are not expecting too much. Jane has a reputation in town as an aggressive mother. If Susan complains about how a teacher or a friend or a coach is not treating her right, Jane takes up her daughter's complaint with the person immediately.

At age five, Susan is an emotional tyrant, but Jane and Matt are too involved in their own particular philosophy of overindulgent parenting to notice. These parents know that their daughter is highly gifted, but they make no attempt to deal with their child's perfectionism, problems with making friends, and demanding nature. In fact, Jane and Matt are unwittingly making their daughter's insecurities more serious and difficult to eventually overcome.

What do these examples demonstrate? Having child-centered expectations is more effective with gifted children because this realistic style of parenting does not feed into the gifted child's perfectionist tendencies. A child-centered approach, as in the first example, teaches children to follow rules that they can understand and cope with and eventually learn to master. When children have a sense of mastery over their world, perfectionistic tendencies are kept under control so that they have inner freedom to explore the world in their own way.

Gifted children with parents who expect too much adult structure and order develop an inadequate and inaccurate sense of themselves because they can never measure up. These children tend to be fearful and shy. They can often be high achievers. But children who have adult rules too early can also be serious underachievers. High achievement is a reaction to trying to please parents, while underachievement is most likely related to anger at their parent's expectations or their own unattainable expectations (see Chapter 6).

A rigidly structured family, such as shown in the second example, is not an optimal environment for the smart perfectionist child. These gifted children develop a poor and inaccurate sense of themselves because their parents have not tuned into their particular interests. Children who lack interests that become passions have a hard time developing a solid identity as teenagers. Children who have not received enough attention from their parents develop poor self-esteem. Often depressed and lost, they seek out negative attention in unrealistic love relationships or drugs.

As seen in the third example, gifted children who have parents who focus on their every need become emotional tyrants who *always* have to be the center of attention. These overindulged children, no matter how smart they are, will have problems with friendships and realistic achievement. Indulged children learn to live in denial as they learn from their parents that they only have to deal with what they want to deal with. Unfortunately, gifted children who are indulged often turn to drugs or sexual enactments to fill up their inner emptiness and lack of discipline.

Teach Your Child That Making Mistakes Is a Part of Life

Gifted children usually want to do everything right the first time. And indeed, they are often good at accomplishing a task correctly and right away. Problems arise when gifted children have to struggle to learn something. Sophisticated parents, or parents who are tuned into their child, know this quirk only too well. For example, I have spoken with parents of an extremely verbal child who made their daughter practice the piano because it was hard for her. They felt, and wisely so, that she needed to be exposed to learning the way most people learn, instead of always just getting a task right the first time.

Perfectionism is the emotional issue that all gifted children must deal with as they develop a sense of themselves. The parents in my support groups spend many hours talking about how to deal with their child's perfectionism. A slogan that became popular in our group was suggested by George, who is a surgeon. George explained to our group that surgeons know that "better is the enemy of good" on the operating table. Trying to perform an operation perfectly can result in all kinds of unnecessary problems. George explained to his son that he only needed to do a good job, because trying to be perfect creates problems of its own. Fortunately, George has a son who could intellectually understand this very important idea. Unfortunately, emotionally processing this idea was difficult for his son, who still would regularly get caught up in trying to do his school work perfectly.

The other parents contributed an array of insights and strategies to the discussion.

Allison: (Explained to her children—endlessly) "Nobody is perfect. The only way to really learn is to make mistakes. And people make mistakes all of the time. Everybody spills!"

Janice: "Once we realized that our son's perfectionism was causing problems for him, we began a conscious program of teaching him that it was okay for something to be difficult, and okay as well to make mistakes. After many storms and tantrums, the lesson seems to be taking—he is now much more willing to try new things even if he isn't obviously good at it from the start, and more willing as well to do a good job, not a perfect one, and move on."

Diana: "Like in all areas, kids really need clear boundaries for their perfectionism. They need to know when they are being realistic (that is, when perfectionism leads to good results) as compared to acting in a way that stifles them and ultimately leads to greater anxiety."

Angela: "I fight the tendency to 'give in' if it's a small issue. If my son refuses to go on to the next task until the current task is done perfectly, I let him know that it's okay to be mad /sad/angry about not having done something completely, and assist him with moving on and leaving the imperfect work as is. This could be an unfinished figure-8 train track, an incomplete picture, a craft project that didn't turn out just right, etc. This will help my son build confidence in dealing with the anxiety he feels when more important tasks are not completed perfectly."

Tanya: "I constantly struggle with this issue and how to deal with it. My daughter has always had an amazing power of concentration from a very early age. She would erase her letters until they were "perfectly" formed to her satisfaction. She would spend a long time working on a drawing and get extremely frustrated if she couldn't make it look up to her standards. Just the other day (at age 7½), she spent over two hours making thank-you cards for her two teachers at the end of the school year."

George: "We are not successful in dealing with our son's perfectionism because he continues to be perfectionist no matter what we do. We have explained to him no one is perfect. We tell him many times about how everybody makes mistakes and life goes on. Only God is perfect. Although he can intellectually pass a pop quiz about perfectionism, his actions do not integrate this knowledge."

Linda: "I deal with my daughter's perfectionism with encouraging words and soothing assurances. I firmly believe that to be a perfectionist is not a handicap, but au contraire, a useful tool. Although childhood perfectionism may perhaps impede some aspects of development, perfectionism in adulthood can lead to excellence. I am cautious about keeping any negativity regarding my daughter's perfectionist traits at bay."

Tony: "My son is sometimes the opposite. With things like spelling
              and writing things down, he's like, 'That's good enough.
              They get the point.' But sometimes he hesitates to do things
              he's not mastered to perfection. I think it helps that I con-
              stantly tell him stories about how bad I am at some things.
              He really likes knowing that I make mistakes."

Remember you can only be a good-enough parent of a gifted
child if you accept that you as a parent will inevitably make some
mistakes, regardless of how smart or devoted you are. No matter
how psychologically attentive you are toward your child, or how
much attention you pay to your child's motivation, and no matter how much thought goes into each decision, sooner or later you
will face issues related to their insistence on understanding and
mastering their own passions.

You will be more effective if you can sit back and listen to the
problems your child is having and not feel the need to immediately
jump in and solve or fix the problem. Talk to your children about
their frustrations. If you allow gifted children to deal with their
own frustrations as a normal part of life, they will be more productive and well adjusted.

Understanding the Deeper Issues Underlying Perfectionism

Sometimes you can talk to your gifted son or daughter until you
are literally ready to scream or just give up. You wonder, "What is
going on in my child's head that she/he can't relax? Why is my
child so obsessed with getting everything right?"

Contemporary psychologists suggest that there are many ways
of looking at what motivates perfectionism in children. One primary trigger that has not been addressed is your own unstated message to your child. You can be an understanding, supportive, and

encouraging parent, but you may not be able to accept all of your child's feelings. Children sense their parents' limitations about tolerating negativity and learn to take care of their parents by being good and well behaved. They unwittingly learn to make parents happy by taking care of them. This often involves ignoring their own painful feelings.

In *The Drama of the Gifted Child,* renowned therapist Alice Miller writes:

> Children can develop a way of *not* experiencing their feelings, for a child can only experience his feelings when there is somebody there who accepts him freely, understands and supports him. If that support is missing, if that child must risk losing the mother's love, he fails to experience his feelings . . . narcissism and the need for perfectionism is from the child's inability to experience his dark and depressing feelings, which the mother, because of her own childhood, cannot accept or tolerate. . . .
>
> Intellectualism is very commonly used as a defense mechanism of great reliability against the fears of abandonment and loss of love. "I must always be good and measure up to the norm, then there is no risk; I constantly feel that the demands are too great, but I cannot change that, I must always achieve more than others."

More simply stated, gifted children may sense on an unconscious level their parents' desire for them to do everything perfectly. This message will contribute to your child's perfectionist tendencies. You are in a catch-22. You need to try not to be perfectionist about your child's perfectionist tendencies, because this won't help. It will just encourage intensity. I am reminded of the perfectionism that played out between my daughter and me. I would say, with honest compassion, "Don't worry, Elizabeth, what you have completed is really beautiful, and it will be well received by (your teacher, your friend, the boss, your boyfriend)."

If my daughter was in an insecure state of mind and her perfectionism was getting the best of her, she would say, "Mom, you are *so wrong*. You are pumping me up. You are the only one who believes in me. I don't care what you say, it's just not right; it's not enough."

I would feel very defeated by this kind of interchange. I learned I needed to let my daughter have her perfectionism tantrums. It was very hard on me. I didn't want her to be in pain. I was trying too hard to be a perfect mother. I had a hard time accepting that I could not protect her from life's hard facts and lessons. I came to understand that overidentifying with my child's pain made her pain more intense.

When your child is struggling with perfectionism, stepping back and taking long, deep breathes helps. You can't get caught up in fixing all your child's issues. Children cannot be protected from unhappy experiences. Children learn from their mistakes and unfortunate events. They become more resilient.

Don't Let Yourself Be Isolated from Other Parents of Gifted Children

Getting stuck alone with all of the problems of raising a gifted child can create serious long-range problems—for you and your child. Parents whose children aren't gifted will have no understanding of what you are going through. Try to find other parents, friends, or family members who are in a very similar situation and you will be more effective with your children.

Some of the members of my parenting group contribute their thoughts and feelings about isolation from other parents:

Tony writes with empathy:

"Parents can be unintentionally judgmental about your child. They see the idiosyncrasies in your child's behavior as possible 'bad parenting' on your part. Other parents may believe that you are not setting enough boundaries for your child, when in fact gifted kids are very curious and often explore beyond the normal boundaries with headstrong determination.

"Other parents can also be envious, and it makes them somewhat uncomfortable to be around you. In turn, you may also isolate yourself after a while, understanding and anticipating more of the same criticalness and envy from other parents.

"Being a parent of a gifted child is like being in a tribe of 1% of the population. Like tribes are comfortable together. There are very few outlets and groups for us. However, there are some gifted parents who do brag cleverly and overtly. I think they are hard to be around. Perhaps most people anticipate that all parents of bright children will be braggarts."

Isabella, a mother of five-year-old twins, writes about her frustrating experiences with others and why she feels isolated.

"I think all parents want their children to be gifted, and when they realize they're not, they become jealous of those parents who have children who excel.

"Many mothers keep their child's giftedness a SECRET. Then they have no outlet and no friends that they can share this secret with, and they are isolated.

"Other parents say behind my back: 'Oh, that parent brags. Oh, that parent thinks her kids are so smart. She pushes her children.' When the gifted kids go to the head of the class, these same parents say it's not important. 'She should be interested in their social development and not just the academic portion.'

"Every step of the way is a battle with teachers, parents, and the principal. And these battles further isolate the mother of gifted children. It's exhausting, and you wonder, when will someone understand, and when will someone care?"

Angela has a slightly different take on why she feels isolated from the other moms. Angela writes:

"Some isolation comes naturally, as the gifted child's mother doesn't participate in the standard conversations around the school when parents complain about kids being held back or room assignments. Conversation about fairness and equity can be of little interest to the gifted child's mom.

"A related problem is the response the gifted mother receives if she speaks up about the need to provide a challenging education for her gifted child in the form of differentiated curriculum, etc. This can quickly form an icy wall between the parents of the gifted children and other parents. Who wants to think about her child being nongifted, much less talk about it with parents of more gifted kids? Hence, the mother of the gifted child can feel isolated."

Mary reflects on her very positive experiences with other mothers. Mary says:

"I personally have never been isolated from any other mothers. I have had the full support of many, many women all through the child-rearing process, and they have been a Godsend to me.

"If anyone were to be faulted for isolating, it would be me. Other mothers have always reached out to me."

Keiko explains how she copes:

"I don't really feel isolated from other mothers. My son found other kids who are gifted to play with, and I made friends with their mothers. I avoid discussing giftedness with mothers who I know won't understand my issues as a parent."

George responds in a similar way as Mary. He says:

"I read about this isolation problem in the books you gave me to read about gifted children in your parenting group. My wife and I talk with you and the teacher. But I have never felt isolated from other parents, because we are only interested in our son's social development when we are with other parents. Our kid is just another child who happens to need extra nurturing for his academic gifts.

"There are those crazy, competitive, overachieving parents trying to make their kids into weird physicists or something like that by putting them into special schools for the highly gifted. They are pushing their kids and projecting on to them their dreams. I believe a child's got to get his own life and his own karma.

"My parents never pushed me in any way They provided a safe environment. That's what I want to give my son. I want to provide stimulation and challenge. My spiritual teachings educate me not to limit others because of my own prejudices. Maybe my values as a parent and my spiritual support keep me from feeling isolated."

Cynthia, an elementary school teacher, does not feel isolated from others. She explains:

"I had other teachers who are parents to talk to about child development. I knew from my experiences as a teacher and my education that my son was not normal. He is exceptional. I used some of the strategies I learned as a teacher to deal with his energy and curiosity. I would talk to other teachers, who would give me tips. There is giftedness in my family and so I could also talk it over with members of my close and extended family."

Laura is concerned about how other mothers' reactions may harm her son.

"It can be awkward having a child who's intellectually ahead of his peers. I remember when Luke's preschool teacher asked me, wide-eyed, if I knew he could read when I picked him up from school one afternoon. Well, of course I did—he'd been reading for months. But I felt like I needed to respond very modestly about it—almost downplaying it—because it's hard to talk about your child's giftedness without feeling like you're coming across like a braggart. Other parents sometimes look shocked when they see him reading or doing math. Some act as though it's odd; other's suggest that he must be a genius; and still others compare their own older children's development to him unfavorably (sometimes in front of their children). So you learn not to talk about it, except among your inner circle. The last thing I want is for Luke to be made to feel different in a negative way."

Avoid Parenting Traps

As the parent of a gifted child, you need to be aware of certain common parent traps. These traps will hinder your child's development and create frustration for the entire family. Be serious about avoiding these misguided ideas.

Parent Trap 1: Gifted Children Raise Themselves

The mothers of nongifted children often will tell you that having a gifted child must be easier because gifted children are so smart, they can manage everything on their own. Most likely, these opinionated parents are jealous that you are the parent of a gifted child, and that is why they are so nonsupportive of your challenges and your burdens.

So what if parents of nongifted children really do believe that gifted children can raise themselves? You know this is not true. You know that gifted children are highly energetic, sensitive and inquisitive. They drain your energy and challenge your sensibility and brain power. Ignoring the advice of jealous parents is not only very advisable, it is a must do!

Parent Trap 2: You Can Raise Your Gifted Child by Yourself

It is very hard to raise a gifted child; support from friends and family is crucial. If you try to raise your child on your own, you will be drained and ineffective. Find a support group or educational group in your community that can help you with understanding your gifted child as well as the day-to-day challenges of raising a very bright child. Enlist the active hands-on help of your spouse or partner. In addition, make sure your partner is involved in making key decisions on school choices, discipline, and enrichment activities. You are sure to get unfortunate results if you think that you can succeed alone!

Parent Trap 3: It Is OK to Brag About Your Gifted Child

Of course you are a proud parent, and you should be. While it is very easy to talk nonstop about your little genius and his or her remarkable behavior, this can be very stressful on your child. It is extremely important to limit your bragging behavior to your therapist, one or two very close friends, or your parents, if they promise not to repeat what you say to their casual acquaintances at the market or shopping mall. Gifted children feel pressured by too much parental bragging, as it creates expectations that they may not be able to live up to. Bragging also creates a false sense of self for your child. You want your child to be who they are, not who they seem to be as defined by their incredible achievements. If not, you will end up with a driven perfectionist child or perhaps a drop-out, or possibly even worse.

Respect your child's privacy. If your child wants to brag about his own accomplishments, that is fine. But when you do the bragging, you inadvertently create pressure and high expectations for further achievements.

Parent Trap 4: Your Child Is So Gifted, School Will Be Easy

Thinking that your child is going to have an easy time at school because he or she is so smart is short-sighted and foolish. Gifted children often have problems at school because they are easily bored in a regular classroom. Or they might actually act dumber so they will have more friends or be more like the other children in the class.

Another common problem that gifted children have at school occurs in subjects or activities that do not come easily for them. Gifted children are used to getting everything right the first time. They have not yet been educated in the art of struggling. It is not unusual for a gifted child to have great difficulty learning simple tasks that do not come naturally to them.

Parent Trap 5: You Should Give Your Child Everything You Did Not Get as a Child

Don't wish for your child what you long for yourself. This is a totally misguided approach to parenting. The psychological label for this type of behavior is *overidentification with your child*. In simple terms, this means that you believe, on some unconscious or preconscious level, that you can relive your life through your child. When you are overidentified with your son or daughter, you think or feel that your child will want what you want. In some instances this may be true, but it's not true in most situations. For example, let's say you were an only child, with all the difficulty that entails in making new friends, and you want your child to have a lot of friends. Your child is shy and likes to play with one friend at a time. You pressure your child to be more outgoing, when it is really not something that he or she enjoys. This will cause stress between you and your child. Both of you will feel dissatisfied with one another. Remember—you are the adult and need to let your children be who they are.

Another example: Because you were very poor as a child, you had only one good pair of shoes and one good dress. To make up for past suffering, you shop constantly for your daughter so that she can have the latest styles and best outfits. Your daughter is not very interested in clothes, as she is a tomboy. She does want to be in style, but she wants to be comfortable in her clothes and to have room for action. You are both frustrated by your efforts to correct the past. You have to learn to let your child live her own life.

Parent Trap 6: There Is a Perfect School in Your Community That Will Meet Your Child's Every Need

Finding the right school for your child is challenging and complicated. Obviously, there is no one school that will work for all gifted children, being that giftedness is so variable. Just look at the different areas giftedness can apply to: music, art, science, and so on.

There is a common myth that there is one great fabulous school on the hill that all gifted children should go to. At this mythical school, though, the rejection rate is high. It is tough to get in, and what will you do if you are rejected?

The reality is that you will have to make a lot of personal choices about your child's education. Focusing on your values, looking at your options, and being realistic about what you can afford will lead to your best decisions about schooling. Working with your child's teachers will always be necessary, as very bright children are hard to educate and need a great deal of special input.

Parent Trap 7: You Must Devote Your Entire Life to Your Energy-Draining Gifted Child

Parents from every generation and every walk of life have fallen into this trap with their gifted children, with unfortunate consequences. The overly catered-to child becomes an emotional tyrant who can't function independently in the world. Devoting your life to your children gives them too much adult power and sense of self-importance, and it leaves you with nowhere to turn when they leave home.

Parent Trap 8: Your Gifted Child Probably Can Run the House Better Than You Can

When you are not exhausted, you know better than this. Very smart children are especially good talkers, expert know-it-alls, and good debaters. They are very convincing, but they are just children, and they should be treated as such. Children should not be allowed to make adult decisions, even if they believe they can.

Parent Trap 9: You Can Solve Every Problem That Comes Your Way

Wrong! Sometimes you have to accept the limitations that you face at your child's school, with your spouse, with your housekeeper,

with the carpool, and with the teachers, and enrichment specialists. You don't have to do everything perfectly. Everyone is behind
the eight ball at one time or another. Even the gifted mother loses
her cool once in a while.

Strive for "Good Enough," Not Perfection

Gifted children usually have gifted and ambitious parents. Unfortunately, the perfectionism of the successful and driven parent
feeds into the perfectionism of the child. If you have to do everything "right" for your child to feel complete inside yourself, your
child will surely suffer. Perfectionism as a style of child-rearing stifles children and makes them angry, anxious, and even defiant.
Most perfectionistic and demanding parents make their children
feel inadequate. Even when you have realistic standards for your
children, you can easily fall into parent traps that distract you
from playing a "good-enough" role as a parent. It is extremely helpful to find people in your community who can support and understand what you are going through.

Think about the following issues that directly relate to your
parenting style:

1. Do you understand where your child is most gifted?
2. Do you understand where your child is having the most
   difficulties?
3. Are you a different parent than your parents? Why? How?
4. Are you overidentified with your child? Why? How will
   you change?
5. What rules or structure do you set up for your family?
   Why have you chosen these rules?
6. How do you deal with your own perfectionism?
7. How do you deal with your child's perfectionism?
8. Do you have as much support as you need from your
   spouse?

9.   Do you talk with other parents who have gifted children?

10. How do you work with your child on difficult tasks? Or in difficult situations?

11. What do you do when others pressure your child?

12. Have you thought about what would be the best school for your child?

13. Do you fall into the common parenting traps for gifted parents?

Practical Advice

Here are some hands-on strategies for dealing with your child's perfectionism:

Play games where chance is emphasized. Games that are not totally dependent on skill teach children that it is OK to lose. Games that involve chance can also help children learn how to be gracious losers and how to play games for fun.

Practice practicing. Find some activity that your child will have to work at that you know is not easy. Music can work well for those who are not musically inclined because any mistakes that are played do not stick around like a drawing or a sculpture.

Emphasize process, not outcome. Ask your child questions like these: How did you come to that conclusion or that next step? What made you decide to use that color? What did you learn from the entire experience?

Be specific with expectations. Gifted children are very literal, so make sure to define and be specific. Explain exactly what you mean by "finishing" the project. Have your child work in small increments of study time to get the most out of it.

Have a sense of humor. Gifted children are already hard on themselves; it is great if you can all laugh together when mistakes are made.

Discuss how mistakes can be good. People learn from their mistakes. Give your child some examples of how you have learned from your mistakes. Demonstrate to your child how you deal with your mistakes. Show your children the ways you are a perfectionist and how you cope with it. Point out common mistakes that you make. Tell stories of mistakes you made while you were growing up.

Set priorities and put things in perspective. Always discuss how relatively important the outcome of a specific task is. Explain to your children that they do not have to get it exactly right the first time.

Set goals. Start by practicing with small goals and gradually make long-range goals. Make sure all goals are realistic and attainable.

Finding the Right School for Your Gifted Child

"School options for the gifted are sadly nonexistent, as is witnessed by the fact that grade acceleration has become a taboo for a great many gifted students. How absurd that a resource as rich as these engaged and imaginative minds is being squandered in an attempt to keep America's classrooms 'equitable.'"   Linda

"I'm happy with the school we chose because our son is unfolding into his own self. The school respects each child's individuality no matter how fast or slow they are working. For example, the teacher saw that our son got bored without being told. She paired him into a higher group which gives him more challenging material. The school and our family form a good partnership. We agree not to push him but to challenge."   George

You are rightly concerned about the education of your gifted child. There are challenges and roadblocks all along the way. Helping your very bright child get the right educational start is truly one of the most essential and priceless gifts that you can give to the child.

Today you are under increasing pressure because you are in competition with countless other parents who also want the best for their children, whether or not they are gifted. More and more parents strive to get their child on the right track very early in life, by carefully selecting which toddler "Mommy and Me" classes to attend with their child. More parents than ever are checking out all the preschools in their neighborhood, attempting to give their child an enriched early childhood education. In the extreme, some parents enroll their children in the "quality" preschools before they are born! These parents wrongly believe that the right preschool will ensure entrance to a good private school and that down the road this school will lead to entrance at a prestigious college. You should understand that the problems of educating a child are far more complicated than choosing the right preschool.

Selecting a kindergarten presents all parents with even more options and opportunities for confusion. And admittance to certain kindergartens is not as easy as getting into preschool. In some instances, it can be more competitive to get a child into the "right" kindergarten than it is to get that same child into college. Later, decisions about middle school and high school confront both students and parents, who will then concern themselves with college admittance.

You may wonder if there is a connection between where your child gets her early education and her future educational opportunities. Of course there is some correlation, but there are no guarantees that the "right school" will produce a self-motivated, productive student. Rather, good parenting is crucial if children are going to form a vision for what they want to become and then develop the skills necessary to achieve their goals.

Looking at Your Educational Options

Clearly, your educational choices are critical and complicated. Some parents have the idea that power and prestige in education can be bought or negotiated, and that a fine education will produce a gifted individual. This false belief permeates the problem of finding the right school placement for your gifted children. The new consumer and power-broker component of education intensifies the distinct challenges parents of gifted children face, because they are fighting for limited spaces with parents who want to buy giftedness.

Let's go back to the question asked in Chapter 1: "Is every child gifted?" The answer is no. But this does not stop ambitious parents from trying to promote their child as gifted. And so the myth that all children are gifted continues to cause problems for educators, who suspect that parents think their child is gifted because it appeals to and feeds into the parents' sense of power and prestige.

What about the child who is truly gifted? There is a general lack of agreement about what gifted children need in a school setting. What is best? A private school? A public school? A religious school? Home schooling? The answer to this question varies from child to child and family to family. Indeed, the differences within the gifted category are as great or greater than the variation between the gifted and nongifted. In other words, because the range of variability among gifted children is so enormous, there is no way to prescribe a gifted education that will work for all children.

Research on how to educate gifted children is truly contradictory. Some educational researchers suggest that a public education is most valuable because it exposes a gifted youngster to different ethnicities and cultures. Public education is available to all children. By definition, public schools are not elitist, but there are hidden forms of discrimination. Within the public school system there are different types of gifted components, ranging from weekly pull-out classes to separate schools for the gifted. These vary from school district to school district and within the school district from school to school. Unfortunately, public gifted education has been very, very neglected in recent years because of the No Child Left Behind Act. This legislation led to an absence of accelerated curriculum and instructional material that is definitely a serious drawback to many gifted children and their concerned parents.

Private schools suffer from elitism because they are open only to children who can meet the entrance criteria. These privately funded schools believe in and can logically support the value of their enriched curriculum for gifted children. Private schools do have more say over what is taught and how it is taught. These schools tend to have a more innovative approach to curriculum, which can be individualized for the students who attend.

Private schools that are exclusively for highly gifted children believe that they provide the most challenging type of education. In highly gifted schools, children are segregated with other very bright children and never need to bother themselves with ordinary learners or lessons. In their formative years, these children are isolated from mainstream children. Often, children in these "hothouses" of intellectual stimulation and expectations burn out from too much pressure.

Religious schools are a different type of private school with a very traditional approach to instruction. Although religious schools can sometimes be closed-minded in their approach to innovative curriculum, they often use the technique of skipping grades to deal with children who are very advanced. Acceleration of gifted children has been shown to have positive effects on intellectual development without the feared negative social and emotional consequences.

The problem with private schools is that they are selective. Private schools, in general, are for wealthy families with gifted children or religious families who subscribe to specific religious and spiritual beliefs. Underprivileged gifted children and just plain folks really have limited access to these schools.

Home schooling is a new trend in education for the gifted. Some people believe that home schooling is a last resort when a child cannot be placed in a highly gifted program or accelerated to the next grade. Others truly believe in home schooling for profoundly gifted children with IQs above 170. Home schoolers generally believe in early entrance to college for gifted children. Home schooling is more prevalent in rural areas.

The debate about the right way to educate a gifted child is long-standing. I can find no perfect type of curriculum that is right for every gifted child. You must choose carefully among your options, keeping in mind what you value in education for your child and what you can afford.

School Placement Depends on the Individual Situation

You can learn about the process of selecting the right school for your gifted child by understanding how other parents evaluate their options early in their child's life. Let's look at five families who take their own unique perspectives into consideration while selecting a school for their gifted son or daughter. Their specific needs for their children demonstrate how unique each family situation really is, and, in turn, what there is about each type of school that is special. You cannot match your child with the right school until you understand what is unique about your child, your family, your values, and expectations for your child.

The Ray Family: Determined to Find the Right School for Their Child

I am reminded of my first phone call and consultation with the Ray family. Mrs. Ray left a message for me on my answering machine. She asked if I could call her back and help her with her four-year-old daughter Claire's placement in elementary school. When I returned her call, Beverly Ray was eager to explain her situation with schools for her daughter. She sounded like she was an extremely articulate and informed parent, as well as warm and concerned. We made an appointment for the entire family to come to my office.

Beverly and Claire arrived early for our meeting. Mr. R.C. Ray was unable to attend because he was tied up on a project at work and sent his regrets. Beverly was an extremely attractive, outgoing, devoted, and energetic mother. Claire was a very bright, adorable, well-dressed child with excellent manners. Claire, like her mother, had a gift for self-expression. Claire carefully explored all of the different toys and games I had in my office, while I talked with her mother. Claire asked me several questions about my office that led me to believe that she was extremely precocious. I began to wonder about how high this child's IQ really was.

Beverly explained to me that she had placed Claire in a small Montessori preschool, Sunshine, near home. Claire was very advanced in doing her numbers and letters and Sunshine allowed her to work at her own accelerated pace. Claire was extremely sociable, and she had lots of friends, Beverly reported. Claire loved school and its many enrichment activities, including gymnastics and ballet. Claire had a loving relationship with her younger brother. The family liked to travel when R.C. was not working. R.C. guarded his time with both of his children on the weekends and he was involved in all family decisions.

I spoke with Beverly about her own educational experiences growing up. She explained that she had gone to small private schools in Switzerland and France until her family moved to a small, well-to-do community in the United States, where she attended public school. Beverly graduated from an excellent university. Her husband had attended public schools and spent a brief time in college. Beverly was more interested in private schools and her husband was more interested in public education. Because Beverly and R.C. could well afford private schools, I suggested that Beverly look at several private and public schools in her extended neighborhood that would provide Claire with an enriched education. I was already sure that Claire was highly gifted and that she would need extra attention and challenge.

Beverly took me seriously and spoke with and toured all of the schools I suggested. She observed the teachers and the students so she could come to her own decisions. I was delighted when Beverly called to tell me about her decision to send Claire to a private school with an individualized approach to education, a diversified curriculum, and an excellent reputation in her community.

What Are School Promotional Materials Really Telling Parents?

Much will depend on what the school means by *individualization*. Will Claire be expected to work alone on academic tasks aimed at developing a skill the teacher thinks Claire should acquire, or does individualizing mean an opportunity for Claire to pursue a study related to her personal interests? How will the school reinforce Claire's outgoing social nature and, at the same time, promote her personal identity? Does addressing individuality lead to self-centered behavioral narcissism, or does it strengthen a desire to share and help others, especially those from diverse backgrounds?

We also want to know more of what this school means by *diversity*. Is it a place where students feel safe to express their different views and know that teacher and peers will listen and learn from each other? In addition to encouraging diversity of ideas, will the school offer opportunities for the student to develop awareness, understanding, and appreciation of cultural differences? How is the school likely to prepare Claire for meaningful future relations with people like and unlike herself? How will Mr. and Mrs. Ray relate to the other parents and faculty at the new school? Will they fit into their new role as parents in a private school? Will R.C. view the school as favorably as his wife, Beverly, does?

Later in this chapter, we'll see what happens when Claire starts school.

The Owen Family: How Does a Learning Challenge Affect School Placement?

I met Michelle Owen at a lecture I was giving on options for elementary education. She called me immediately after my lecture to schedule a consultation about school placement for her son, Noah. Michelle told me that Noah had been diagnosed with autistic spectrum disorder at one and a half. Noah had participated in all of the latest early behavioral intervention programs, which included speech therapy, a special therapeutic afternoon school, and a shadow teacher at a regular preschool. I estimated that the regional center that worked with this family had spent approximately $100,000 a year on Noah's extra developmental needs.

Michelle wanted to come to our first consultation with her husband to explain in more detail Noah's strengths and limitations and the extent of the treatment he had received. Michelle and David Owen were young, attractive, well-spoken, and serious professionals, who both worked full time. Michelle seemed to have more freedom to leave the workplace and attend meetings regarding her children. David seemed a little more sure of himself as to what he might want for his son, while Michelle was quite unsure of what would be a good kindergarten placement for her son. I wondered how the early diagnosis of autistic spectrum would affect school placement.

Noah, who was five years old, was making excellent progress with his socialization skills. Michelle had been told by several psychologists that Noah was gifted and that this might be contributing to his shy nature. His shyness was understandable, as he had been very protected by all of the behavioral intervention he had experienced in his short life. In our first consultation I suggested that he be allowed more independence and more unstructured time to prepare him for his transition to kindergarten. I shared with Michelle and David my concern that the "good" private schools did not like to take children who had never been in preschool without a shadow teacher. Or, more honestly, the "good" private schools did not take children who were not "problem free." By contrast, public schools were eager to have children who had shadow teachers because it provided the classroom teacher with an extra set of hands and eyes. Both parents were concerned that the public school in their neighborhood was too large for Noah. They wanted a small private school environment in their home community.

I asked Michelle and David about their own educational experiences growing up as a way to understand their views of education and schooling. Both parents had attended public schools throughout their entire educational careers. Each of them had a graduate degree from a public university. I wondered if they wanted a different experience for their son, or if they were really concerned about the quality of public education.

I meet with Noah and Michelle at the next meeting. Noah is a wonderful and warm child with bright reddish-orange hair and intense blue eyes like his mother. He was slightly slow to interact with me, and he watched his mom carefully as I talked to her. Noah was careful and very serious in his approach to drawing and playing with blocks. Although Noah's play was creative, his behavior lacked spontaneity. My immediate impression was he had outgrown his diagnosis of autistic spectrum disorder, which is common for some children who get a great deal of appropriate behavioral intervention.

I suggested that Noah go to preschool without a shadow teacher. Michelle was very concerned about whether he would be able to handle the social demands of preschool without the extra help of a shadow teacher. At the same time, she was able to step back and see that Noah was doing better after all of the hours of special therapy he had received. But she was still afraid to go ahead and let him be more independent from his treatment team. Michelle was trying to be hopeful that by the fall Noah would be able to attend a "good" private school, as she saw this as an advantage over public school.

I spent many intense hours speaking with Michelle about the autistic spectrum disorder label that Noah had been given as an infant and toddler. I was convinced that Noah was no longer "on the spectrum," and the treatment team that had worked with him for over three years agreed with me. I needed to help Michelle get rid of Noah's label. Unfortunately for everyone involved, Michelle hung onto the diagnosis as if it was her burden to bear forever. And so, I began my mission to educate her about the hazards of labeling children.

The Dangers of Labeling a Child

One danger of labeling a child with a disorder is that the label may prevent people from seeing that the child no longer matches the label. If Noah has profited from the behavioral intervention, perhaps we should drop the label and think of opportunities that are more appropriate for the new Noah. When I met with Noah, I definitely felt that looking at Noah as a child who had the issues of a highly gifted child was more beneficial to his overall education than labeling him on the autistic spectrum.

We know that negative prophecies are harmful because of their self-fulfilling nature and that positive expectations can work wonders. A child who is labeled as a problem will surely have problems at school. A child who is labeled as bright, creative, or talented will soar.

Parental reliance on institutional diagnoses and interventions raises the risk of failing to truly understand the individual child. The school may not know what the child can do in a home situation. The school's categorizing of children and standardizing solutions to a child's problems also has a margin of error, although they probably won't admit this. More often than not, the diagnosis is not reliable over time and the standardized treatment is ineffective.

Labeling has increased with the medicalization of education. The listing of deficits grows ever longer—autistic spectrum disorder, attention deficiency, hyperactivity, dyslexia disorders, and the like. Negative terms that characterize children are often harmful, but positive attributes can do a world of good.

Labeling by intelligence is likewise controversial. Intelligence (IQ) tests aim at assessing the student's ability to reason, to understand abstractions, and to solve problems. IQ tests differ from school tests of knowledge and skills that measure vocabulary and general information.

However, alternative measures of intelligence are available to show strengths of learners. Howard Gardner has proposed at least eight intelligences—linguistic, logical-mathematical, musical, bodily kinesthetic, special, inter- and intra-personality, existential, and naturalistic. Daniel Coleman has written on the importance of emotional intelligence, a critical aspect of social intelligence. Robert Sternberg has developed assessment devices to measure what he thinks intelligence is—analyzing, solving problems, and thinking critically.

We'll see what happens with Noah and his parents later in this chapter.

The Herrera Family: Should the School Reflect the Family's Cultural and Religious Values?

I met Anita Herrera at an open house where I was speaking about developing a gifted child's potential. After asking me many questions about her son, she asked for my business card. Anita was a tall Hispanic woman with three young children, ages one, three, and nearly five. She described herself as an entrepreneur. She ran a small family catering business with her older brothers and mother. Her business was successful, which allowed Anita to make her own schedule. Her husband, Raul Herrera, was an accountant for a large private company.

Anita called me later and said that she and Raul would like to talk with me about the arguments they were having about the right school for their son Armando, who was soon to be five. Armando had already been tested by a psychologist in their community, and had scored 171 (IQ) on the Stanford-Binet. I was eager to make an appointment with the family because they appeared to be quite animated and informed about their choices. I imagined that we would have plenty to talk about.

Raul and Anita arrived at my office in the middle of one of their long battles over the right school for Armando. Raul was a tall, handsome man, who was as well spoken as his wife. Raul explained to me that he had attended Catholic schools all of his life and wanted his children to have the same type of educational experience. Anita had also attended Catholic schools during her educational career, and she wanted to give her children a different kind of experience.

Anita wanted her children to go to the excellent up-to-date public school in their neighborhood, which had a program for gifted children. Anita had checked out this school. She was impressed that parents were very involved in the classroom activities. Students from different ethnicities were bused in from all over the city, because the school had an excellent reputation as a cultural melting pot. Anita was sold on this school. She wanted her children to be exposed to more diversity than she had experienced growing up. Anita thought that the public school had better teachers, a more "modern" curriculum, and better opportunities for enrichment for her gifted son.

I could easily see that the battle over schools between Anita and Raul was serious. Each one held on to their strong opinions. I tried to get them to see each other's point of view. I talked about the value of a religious education and the value of a public education. I mentioned the fact that gifted children had special educational needs. All of my additional talking did not resolve anything.

I asked what their son's preference might be. This question helped Anita and Raul think more deeply about their opposing positions. Armando was an artistically inclined child who loved to draw and paint. He tended to be shy in social situations because he had always been with his own family and extended family. He had a few very good friends; and even at five he was not interested in being popular. Armando liked math and he loved to read. He was well behaved at his Catholic preschool.

When Anita and Raul left my office, I was totally unsure about what decision they would make. I hoped that the time I spent with them had helped them think more deeply about their decision. I hoped I had impressed upon them that a child with a 171 IQ needs special educational challenges.

Is a Traditional Education More Important Than a Contemporary Education?

Raul and Anita represent two very different philosophies. Raul seems to think that early schooling should acquaint students with ideas that have perennial value and have withstood the test of time. The development of moral character might also be a major consideration in Raul's choice. It is likely that Raul wants Armando to be educated so he will apply himself to useful tasks, putting effort before his own interests. In contrast to Anita, Raul sees the latest curriculum fad, "organizational technology," as less important than depth of studies that can be related to contemporary problems.

Anita appears to be both present and future oriented. She is aware of the multicultural context and the uncertainty of the future. Like the progressive thinker and educator John Dewey, Anita seems to believe that the best preparation for the future is to get the most meaning from the present. She is open to participation in the education of Armando, which may reflect an understanding that knowledge is best acquired through projects with others, communities of learners, dialogue-shared experiences, and opportunities for Armando to "create himself" as the finest, contributive, joyful person he can become. Anita wants a school that will attend to Armando's attitudes and readiness instead of carrying out prescriptive lessons that regulate time and sequence, limiting the breadth of what is to be experienced.

We'll check back on Armando's situation later in the chapter.

The Thornwood Family: Seeking a Traditional Gifted Private Education at Any Cost

Rene Thornwood called me to set up an appointment to have her son Ronald evaluated for a highly gifted private school in her community. I asked if I could meet with her and her husband before working with her son. Mrs. Thornwood explained in a lyrical Southern accent that her husband was an important executive at a very successful entertainment company. He was never able to attend meetings regarding their son. I did not share with her that I was a little taken back by her responses, which implied that her husband was unavailable to tend to his son's schooling issues. I asked to meet with her alone first. Rene was very gracious and flexible, and she took my first available appointment.

Rene's personal assistant called to let me know that Rene was on her way to my office. And sure enough, Rene arrived exactly on time for our meeting. Rene was an elegantly dressed, attractive, older mother. She explained to me that she had grown up in a wealthy Southern family. She had attended prestigious private schools and colleges. Her chosen profession was architecture, but she was at present doing interior design for large hotel corporations. Rene had met her husband, Gary, when she was doing interior designing in Switzerland. She was in her late thirties when they married. And at the age of 45 she had a son. I gleaned from the conversation the Mr. Thornwood did not seem to have a deep commitment to parenting, but financially supported his family in grand style. The Thornwoods lived in a large mansion with its own park, swimming pool, tennis courts, and many servants. I got the impression that the servants helped Rene raise Ronald.

Rene talked to me at great length about the "genius" in her family. Her parents and relatives were all highly successful doctors and lawyers. Rene was sure that Ronald had inherited her genetic inclinations. In spite of her clarity about her son's genius, she needed to have an evaluation done to apply to a school for the highly gifted. Ronald was attending a preschool that was academic. There was no question in her mind that a traditional gifted private school education was right for Ronald.

I made an appointment to meet with Ronald to evaluate him for entrance to a private kindergarten. When Rene brought Ronald to my office, she was dressed in jeans and a polo shirt and she looked more like a mom to me. Ronald was wearing shorts and a shirt. Ronald seemed to be "just a kid," who was anxious being in a strange office doing strange tasks. Actually, Ronald seemed a little awkward to me, and I had a hard time connecting with him as he was easily distracted. I had difficulty completing the evaluation. Rene did not help me as she pressured Ronald to respond, which further distracted him.

When I finally completed the testing I was exhausted from all of Ronald's extra energy. I was sure that Ronald should attend a more nurturing developmental school rather than the pressure-cooker gifted school. I made an appointment to meet with Rene alone.

In our last meeting I was unable to get my point of view across to Rene, who really just wanted her child's IQ score for the prestigious school. I tried to be frank with Rene and I suggested that her husband spend more time with his child. This advice fell on deaf ears, as did my suggestion that a developmental school would be better until Ronald could develop his power of concentration. The Thornwoods wanted a traditional private highly gifted education for their son, no matter what the cost.

Is Individualized Education Important for Gifted Children?

Parents and educators have to look at what an academic program means. Traditionally, academic programs emphasized content, usually as separate school subjects such as math, English, science, or related disciplines. This content was to be acquired by the student through study and participation in recitations the teacher presented. The teacher then questioned students and confirmed or enlarged upon their responses. This very rigid and directed approach is outdated when it comes to working with gifted children.

A new academic program is being promoted by the National Academy of Scientists and the National Research Council of Education. This program emphasizes students' deep understanding of key concepts in academic fields and the ability to use these concepts in many situations. The new academics have these features:

- ❏ Students engage in real-world problems or unsolved problems in a given special field.
- ❏ Teachers in the new academic program are facilitators, helping students formulate their questions or problems to be addressed.
- ❏ Students plan and collect data in their investigation, and engage in data analysis and interpretation, presenting their findings and recommendations before an appropriate audience.
- ❏ Students are expected to work collaboratively, sharing ideas and solutions in small and large groups.

Clearly this new academic program for learning is best suited for gifted children.

We will revisit Ronald's entrance into kindergarten later in this chapter.

The Green Family: Meeting Their Child's Needs Through Home Schooling

Nora Green called me on the phone to schedule a school consultation for her five-year-old daughter, Kathy. Mrs. Green explained to me that since Kathy was able to talk she had asked questions all day long. She loved learning, and she seemed to soak up knowledge. Kathy had started reading at age three. She attended early private kindergarten. By the time she was ready for public kindergarten, Kathy was working two years above the other children in the class. Mrs. Green was certain that Kathy would be bored in public school.

My evaluation of Kathy merely reaffirmed her giftedness and officially qualified her for the public gifted program and other satellite gifted programs such as Johns Hopkins Center for Talented Youth (CTY).

Mrs. Green explained to me that she had spoken with all of the public schools in the relatively small community where she lived. These schools had policies against acceleration. Administrators told Mrs. Green that they would be unable to provide any gifted education until Kathy was in third grade. Private schools in the area were not openminded about gifted children. The highly gifted schools in her community were too pressured and structured for Kathy. These parents felt as if they were forced out of public and private school early. They made a practical decision to pursue home schooling. It seemed like the only way to meet Kathy's needs.

Mrs. Green has done extensive research on home schooling for gifted children. She shared with me that gifted home schooling was very different than religious home schooling. Mothers who have gifted children create online networks to share useful tools and teaching strategies. Indeed, there were virtual communities for parents of gifted children.

Kathy spoke with me about working with her teacher/mother on reading, math, and science. Kathy enjoys home schooling. She also attends a number of enrichment activities and has regular play dates with other gifted children at the local parks.

Mrs. Green promised to get back to me later in the school year with a report on how Kathy was doing with her home schooling. We'll check back later in the chapter.

Positives and Negatives of Home Schooling

The benefit of home schooling is in the selection of a curriculum that will meet your child's particular strengths and weaknesses. Choosing the right method for your child, from a very structured "school-at-home" approach to a more relaxed structure, is possible. Parents have the freedom to combine multiple methods and curricula. A wealth of information is available on the possibilities.

Advocates of home schooling believe that there is no one cookie-cutter approach that works for all gifted learners because of the asynchronous learning needs of gifted children. The biggest advantage of home schooling is flexibility of curriculum and instruction. However, learner-friendly materials and outside classes and groups that provide social interaction can be a lot of work for the parent. Clearly home schooling is not for the faint of heart. Industrious stay-at-home moms and dads are most successful with this highly individualized approach. Even with highly motivated parents, however, the gifted child is sheltered from the daily rigors of school life that teach children about living with others who are different from themselves.

Common Educational Issues

The common educational issues that the families in this chapter face are representative of what you and other parents of gifted children face.

1. What is the right school for my gifted child?

2. How will the school perceive my child's special needs?

3. Is a traditional education more valuable that a more progressive one?

4. How should I explain to the teacher or the new school my child's unique strengths as a learner?

These issues puzzle and concern most parents. Understanding and acknowledging your own family values and expectations is the first step in making an informed decision about how to select the right school for your child. In other words, you have to be deliberate and honest about what you value in an education and what expectations you have for your child's school. The second step is to find out as much as you can about educational options and opportunities. Every school is unique. The school you select will have a set curriculum and standards for your child. Remember, you are the consumer. As the buyer, you should be aware of what you are getting yourself into.

Let's look at what happened to the Ray family, the Owens, the Herreras, the Thornwoods, and the Greens when their children started kindergarten. Their experiences will illustrate the complexity of the problems in finding the "right school" for your gifted child. *And you will see from these illustrations that when your plans don't work out as well as you expected, your child will still be able to get an excellent education.*

The Rays: A Private School Is Not Always As Described in Promotional Materials

The first day of school arrives. Claire has a new beautiful school wardrobe. Beverly is totally happy with her decision for at least 24 hours. And then she begins to worry. At the new private school, parents are not allowed to cross over the imaginary line that separates the parking lot drop-off from the school. The parents are told not to ask any questions about how their child is doing for two weeks.

Beverly tries to be patient with their new school rules and stays out of the teacher's way. But this is hard for Beverly because she has been an active participant at Claire's Montessori preschool. Following the rule to not ask questions becomes less bearable when Claire starts to complain that school is "too easy" for her. Claire tries to tell her mother everything that goes on in the classroom. Beverly is enraged that the school's promotional materials (e.g., tours and parent–child interviews) do not seem to resemble what actually goes on in the classroom. There is no individualized learning at this private school; rather, all of the children are expected to complete the same work together like little robots, or so it appears. Where is the emphasis on creativity or self-expression? Beverly fears that Claire is not going to be challenged.

Claire gets upset about going to school and starts to get headaches and stomachaches. Claire ends up in the nurse's office so that her mom can pick her up and take her to McDonald's. Mom is ultimately more interesting than school, even though Claire loves her school friends. Formal conversations with administrators lead nowhere. Administrators who seemed open and enlightened at first have become arbitrary monarchs who humiliate families who do not follow their needs. Claire is taken out of this private school and placed in the neighborhood public school with a gifted enrichment component.

Claire is relieved to be back in her own neighborhood. Beverly is delighted to once again have contact with the teachers and the other parents. Claire makes an excellent transition to public school and she makes new friends. Claire is the top reader in class. Beverly takes a break from her worry about Claire.

The Owens: Public School Is Able to Meet the Gifted Child's Needs

The Owen family applies to six private schools. Each of these applications takes hours of preparation. There are interviews, tests, and school visits for each private school, and they are time-consuming and costly. In the end, Noah does not make the cut at any of the private schools. He is placed on six waiting lists. Mr. and Mrs. Owen are very frustrated and disappointed. Michelle rightly believes that the problem with acceptance is related to Noah's previous diagnosis of autistic spectrum disorder and the behavioral interventions he has received. Michelle and David experience prejudice as they discover that private schools only accept children who do not have any noticeable or documented learning issues or special needs.

With a heavy heart and no other options, Michelle and David send Noah to the neighborhood local school, where special services will be provided for Noah if necessary. Fortunately, Noah does very well at the public school without the aid of a shadow teacher. He loves his new kindergarten class and makes friends easily. His teacher is warm and accommodating. Noah is excited about what he is learning. He wants to learn more! Michelle's worst fears, that public education is uncaring and substandard, are unfounded. The public school teachers are very astute, and immediately pick up on Noah's giftedness. Accommodations are made at the neighborhood school to meet Noah's needs for academic challenge. Noah tells his parents he loves public school and wants to stay until he is ten years old.

The Herreras: Parental Conflicts Resolved over Public Education

Mr. and Mrs. Herrera are in conflict about the importance of a traditional religious education. Mrs. Herrera gives in at the last moment and agrees to put their son in a Catholic school. The application arrives too late. There are no openings at the Catholic school. Armando is sent to the local public school, which was his mother's first choice to begin with.

Armando, because he is so shy, has a slow start in kindergarten. Many meetings take place between the parents and teachers. Armando is evaluated by the school psychologist, who immediately picks up that Armando is very bright and can be bored easily. The school psychologist thinks that Armando is unchallenged in his kindergarten class. For most of the day, Armando is left in kindergarten class for socialization, but he is pulled out and taken to first grade for reading every day. Armando begins to like going to school. He is excited about the new challenges he faces in his classrooms on a daily basis. After a month and a half, Armando is making an excellent transition to kindergarten.

Anita and Raul are patient with the administration at their neighborhood school. Both parents are calm and cooperative with the teaching staff. The aura of cooperation seems to help their son feel comfortable with his new school and new friends. Raul and Anita give up their battle over what they think is right and deal with their son's needs.

The Thornwoods: Changing Schools in Mid-Semester

Rene does not give up her insistence that Ronald attend the private gifted school in her neighborhood. Rene and her husband Gary are very delighted when Ronald is admitted. They know that this private school is very status elite and it has a reputation for only taking the smartest kids in town. Rene ignores my warning that this school may be too structured and too pressured for her son.

Ronald has a difficult time adjusting to the private gifted school because the teachers are very strict. There is very little time for play.

Ronald has to learn to dot his *i*'s and cross his *t*'s, even though this is a boring activity for a kindergarten child. To make matters worse, the school is not a friendly place. The children and their parents are very competitive with one another. Ronald senses the pressure. He seems to retreat into himself when he feels he is not at the top of his kindergarten class.

The private school psychologist suggests that Ronald see a child therapist in order to find out what is troubling him. Does Ronald have ADD? Is he depressed? Mrs. Thornwood takes Ronald to a well-respected clinician in her community, who also suggests that Ronald is feeling pressured and trapped at school. The doctor suggests a more developmental and progressive private school where Ronald can be a child and learn at his own pace. Mr. and Mrs. Thornwood finally get this message. Ronald goes to a small, child-centered private school. With care and attention given to his intellectual and emotional strengths, Ronald begins to blossom.

The Greens: Home Schooling as a Viable Alternative

Mr. and Mrs. Green design a personalized education plan for their daughter. Mrs. Green uses the local library, online Internet services, and support groups for home schoolers. Kathy enjoys working with her Mom. She has regular play dates, and she is enrolled in music and dance classes. She continues to excel academically. Kathy attends a summer group for gifted children with other home schoolers.

Mr. and Mrs. Green continue to reevaluate the local public and private schools, because they remain concerned that home schooling does not provide enough socialization for their daughter. As of today, they continue to home-school Kathy because they cannot find a better academic alternative in the public and private sector in this neighborhood.

What to Look for When Seeking a School for Your Gifted Child

The families discussed in this chapter all gave serious thought to what they were looking for in a school for their gifted son or daughter. These parents had a plan of action that they followed with positive and negative results. Some initial plans were revised. The experiences of these families teach us the following:

- ❑ A plan of action for school choice is critical. And this plan may have to be revised.

- ❑ You must take into consideration what is unique about your family and your child's strengths as a learner.

- ❑ Realize that it is very possible that you and your spouse may have different values and goals for your child's education. Try to work out your differences through compromise so this does not hamper you from making the best decision you can make about your child's education.

- ❑ Look at the advantages of public schools, which would include:

  Diversity of students
  Special services for all children with special needs
  More access for parents in the classroom
  Free tuition
  Structured gifted programs
  Peer interaction with children in the neighborhood

- ❑ Look at the advantages of private schools, which include:

  Smaller classes
  A more enriched, refined, focused, and developed curriculum
  Special enrichment classes in arts, science, language, theater, sports, and music
  A more homogenous parent body
  More personal attention and confidentiality given to family issues
  Less troublesome safety concerns

- ❏ No matter what school you choose, prepare yourself for unforeseen problems, which can be addressed through dialogue with the school of your choice.
- ❏ Remember, your voice is important. Make sure it gets heard.

Some Important Points to Keep in Mind

School choice involves compromise. The first issue you face when dealing with school placement for your smart child is the reality that there is no perfect school for your child or the family. You will have to compromise in one way or another. For example, it is very unusual to find a public school in your neighborhood that your child can walk to where the curriculum is innovative enough to meet a gifted child's special needs. Private schools and religious schools are costly and usually involve a commute. The demands of home schooling are enormous. Your final decision will always involve compromise.

Determine how your child is gifted. You need to understand your gifted child's strengths and problem areas and make sure the teacher understands and works with both. This is an ongoing process. You cannot understand the extent of your child's giftedness in one hour with a psychologist, or even one year with a teacher.

Giftedness is a profound quality that requires continual understanding and attention. If your child has an IQ between 132 and 145, then he/she is gifted. This score is in the 98th percentile of all children in a statistical sample. Gifted children have more school options and fit more easily into a regular classroom. Highly gifted children (145+) are more difficult to educate. Scores above 145 are in the top 99th percentile. Often highly gifted children are home schooled or accelerated.

Details are important. Gifted children have asynchronous development—uneven patterns of development. They very often need challenge for their talents and other types of intervention in their areas of weakness. When your child is evaluated for giftedness, be sure to ask the evaluator about your child's specific intellectual potential, personality development, self-concept, learning styles, achievement, and interests. Having this detailed information will help you communicate with the teacher about your child's educational options. Teachers have invaluable insights as well, so listen to what they have to say.

Dealing with the school will be an ongoing challenge. When you do your best to find a school that meets your child's needs, you will have completed step one. There are many stairs left to climb. Realize that dealing with your son's or daughter's school will be an ongoing challenge. Some years will be calm and focused on learning, while other years will be more difficult because of peer problems, teacher–child misunderstandings, or specific academic challenges. Challenges will continue throughout your child's educational experience. We'll explore this in more detail in the next section.

Learn How to Deal with Your Child's School

Let's look at some examples of issues you will face with your child's school and how you can best handle them.

Work with the Teacher

Probably the most important factor in the school environment is your child's teacher. The teacher is the human element. The teacher is the nurturer of your child's intellectual and emotional growth and social development. Never underestimate the teacher's pivotal role. It is quite important that the teacher and your child have some rapport—some intellectual and emotional connection.

Often, teachers and students don't get along. This can lead to serious conflicts between the parents and child and the teacher. This is a very difficult problem. Miraca Gross, a well known teacher of gifted children, writes:

> As a teacher and academic working in gifted education, I have become sadly familiar with the cutting down to size of children who develop at a faster pace or attain higher levels of achievement than their age-peers. Perhaps these children offend our egalitarian principles and our sense of what is fit. Perhaps they threaten us as teachers; few of us encounter, with perfect equanimity, a young child whose capacity to learn is considerably greater than our own. Perhaps they are what we would wish to be, and are not. Perhaps they merely irritate us; gardening would be so much easier if all children progressed at the same rate. For whatever reason, intellectually gifted children are, more often than not, held back in their learning to conform to the pace of other children in their class. In Australia the practice is so explicitly recognized that it even has a special name: 'cutting down the tall poppies'.*

Here are some comments and observations on this issue from some of the parents in my group.

Janice: "Highly gifted children pose a real challenge to teachers, and not all teachers are prepared to meet that challenge. It is very easy to misdiagnose the learning difficulties that often accompany a high degree of giftedness—boredom can be mistaken for attention deficit, or the desire for efficient shortcuts perceived as cognitive difficulty.

"Gifted children are also often sensitive and pessimistic, and a teacher's attempts to correct and instruct may be misperceived by the gifted child as hostile and unreasonable.

*Gross, Miraca. Small poppies: Highly gifted children in the early years. *Roeper Review,* The Roeper School 1999 Vol. 21, No. 3, pp. 207–214.

The result is sometimes a disastrous downward spiral when the teacher tries to 'fix' the gifted child by demanding conformance and focus beyond the child's ability, leaving the child to react by withdrawing or challenging the teacher, causing the teacher to try still harder to 'fix' the child and elicit 'normal' performance. Unhappiness all around results."

Keioko: "Because my son is high maintenance, he gets bored easily and daydreams. The teacher has to wake him up sometimes. Otherwise, he will be an underachiever or class clown. Parents can't be there all the time. The teacher is a guide."

Angela: "The teacher controls the environment that either encourages or discourages your child's interest in learning. However obvious this may seem, the results of teacher actions can have great impact even relative to actions that seem quite minor.

"For example, the seating arrangement chosen by the teacher can work actively to support or diminish interest in learning. A bright, introverted child seated next to the loud, hyperactive child may cause the quiet child to feel intimidation, anxiety, or it may destroy the introverted child's ability to appropriately engage in the classroom activities. Of course this seating arrangement may help the teacher because the introvert probably doesn't engage in the negative behavior, therefore limiting its contagious tendency. The arrangement may even help the loud child focus a little better, but the teacher's decision to use the introverted child in this way can have a strong negative effect for that bright child for the life of the offending seating arrangement, a school year, or possibly much longer.

"Additionally the teacher may influence your child's self-esteem through verbalized and nonverbal feedback, and the health of a child's self-esteem is known to have significant effects in family, educational, and social life."

Tony: "You want the teacher to be invested in your child's well being. Throughout the school day there are trade-offs the teacher makes which may benefit or hurt your child. If too many of the decisions are in favor of ease, 'having all the kids on the same page,' focusing on academically challenged children, standardized test scores, and the teacher's physical or mental test, then the outcome of the school year could be significantly impaired by these trade-offs. On the other hand, a teacher focused on helping your child happily achieve to the level of his potential, with the stamina and knowledge of how to make this happen, can make a lasting impression that can significantly benefit the child for years to come."

Mary: "Why is the teacher so important? (1) Your child will spend an average of 20 to 30 hours a week with this person. They had better be the correct teacher for your child. This is not a tricky answer. It is wholly serious. Especially if your child has special needs and is gifted. (2) The teacher must be smart—smart enough to catch on to the 'slippery' behavior of the very intelligent child. They will try and can pull anything on anybody and everyone. The teacher must have tremendous acuity. Juxtaposed to this—children who are highly gifted and have special needs are highly sensitive and vulnerable. They might need special attention and it might not be easy to figure out what they need. (3) The parents of the highly gifted are generally the same as their children but all grown up with none of the coping skills and considerations we are trying to give our gifted children. We as parents can be real pains in the ass. The teacher must bridge us all. So give them perks and presents."

Tanya: "My daughter is very sensitive to personalities so who the teacher is matters. It affects her comfort level, which in turn affects how hard she works in class. This includes a range from tackling harder work to 'dumbing' herself down.

"It is also important to have a teacher that really understands each child. That teacher can tell when my daughter is dumbing herself down, being distracted, or taking the easy path to avoid more challenging work. The teacher needs to be keenly aware of each child's abilities and help them live up to their capabilities."

Make Personal Connections Within the School Community

The school you select for your child will provide an important social structure for your child and your family. It will be your new extended family and community. Try to get involved in some aspect of your child's school that is interesting for you and, in turn, is helpful to the school as a whole. By becoming involved at your child's school, you will meet other parents, teachers, and administrators who will help you and your child make a successful transition to the new school and its community. You will learn from the members of your new community valuable parenting lessons and strategies that will make you a more effective parent.

Prepare Yourself for the Issues of Homework

Be clear about your expectations for your child's homework activities. Make homework a priority as soon as possible, so that your child will be prepared to learn the responsibility of completing school work. Check your child's homework at a regular time every day. Realize immediately that smart children have a hard time with homework that is boring. You will need to work through problems of boredom and the need for highly stimulating work. Parents are responsible for figuring out how to get the child to do more tasks.

To eliminate some homework issues, find a school that is not exclusively focused on grades. When an opportunity comes up, talk with the teacher about how sensitive gifted children can be and how negatively sensitive they are to any negative comments.

Try to explain the meaning of school and homework to your child. Play games with your child about his homework when it is difficult. Make a list of next steps to try in solving the problem. This will hopefully circumvent your child's perfectionist tendencies.

Think About Your Child's Peer Group

Gifted children have unique socialization issues, which will be discussed in more detail in the next chapter. It is very important to make sure your child has friends to play with several afternoons a week and on the weekend. If your child is having problems establishing friendships, try to understand why. Talk to your child's teachers to get insights and suggestions on who at school might be a good playmate.

Do not let your child become isolated. Find enrichment classes that reflect your child's interests and then help him or her make friends within this group. Involve your child in group-centered athletics. Remember, the latest research suggests that gifted children are likely to make friends who are older than they are.

The Need for Enrichment and Acceleration

Gifted children need enrichment in the areas of their special talents and interest. You will need to develop a sense of what really challenges your child and makes him or her feel confident about his or her unique identity. Carefully choose enrichment activities that will help your child evolve into a well-rounded person who has distinct talents. Be careful not to overload your child with too many extra activities. Some parents can get too intense about exposing their children to too much at once.

The latest research suggests that acceleration is an educational intervention that allows gifted children who are working at a faster pace to move as quickly as they can through a traditional curriculum. Acceleration can be an individualized approach as well as a large- or small-group approach.

Acceleration does not mean pushing a child. It does not mean forcing a child to learn advanced material or to interact with older children before he or she is ready. Indeed, it is the exact opposite.

Acceleration is about appropriate educational planning. It is about matching the level of complexity of the curriculum with the readiness and motivation of the child.

Acceleration is sometimes criticized because it separates students from their peer age group. There is a lack of empirical research to support the notion that separation from age/grade level peers leads to adjustment or achievement problems. The issue of acceleration is very complicated, and acceleration should be individualized for each child. The brighter the gifted child, the more likely that acceleration will be necessary. Highly gifted children with an IQ above 160 are more likely to benefit from this type of intervention than a child with an IQ of 132+.

Meeting the Educational Challenge

Finding the right school for your gifted child is a challenging task, which requires you to consider everything from making a realistic plan to checking out your options to filling out the application, seeing the school, and making a choice. Consider what you value in education.

1. What kind of educational experience do you want for your child?
2. Are you interested in a more innovative curriculum that is child-centered and project-centered or a traditionally focused school? Why?
3. Should the school you choose look at your child's developmental readiness? Why?
4. Do you believe all children learn at the same rate?
5. Do you want the same type of educational experience for your son or daughter as you had? Why or why not?
6. Do you want the opposite type of education that you experienced? Why or why not?

Take into account practical matters such as:

1. How much can you afford?
2. How much time will it take to get your child to school?
3. Will your spouse be able to help you with your driving arrangements?
4. Will your child attend the neighborhood school and walk?

In your plan of action for deciding which school is best for your child, you need to consider all types of issues, from distance to cost to educational philosophy. Remember, schools promote values. Make sure you choose a school that will reflect your beliefs about education and schooling.

In addition, continue to reevaluate on a regular basis how well your child is doing in school. Work with the teachers.

Interactive Tools to Help You

Think about and use the following interactive tools to help you understand and draw conclusions about your unique family needs and what kind of school you want for your child.

My Priorities in Choice of School

The school's: *1 (Less)–5 (Most Important)*

1. Reputation   _____
2. Convenience to parents' schedule,
   e.g., transportation   _____
3. Modern learning technologies and methodologies   _____
4. Influence on morality and character   _____
5. Networking with affluent parents and children   _____
6. Reinforcement of family values   _____
7. Multicultural experience   _____
8. Alternative views of world   _____
9. Response to special needs   _____
10. Emphasis on math and reading   _____

Preliminary Evaluation of a School Under Consideration

Make site observations, with interviews, and contact other parents and other students attending the school.

Which Best Characterizes this School?

NEW VIEWS OF LEARNING	OLD VIEWS OF LEARNING
Language	
Taught through social conversation.	Taught by modeling proper academic speech.
Young child's speech is elaborated upon (e.g., "big dog" teacher—"Yes, the big dog is jumping.").	Teacher affirms or corrects the child's response.
Content	
Focus is on *how* to learn—how to ask questions and act in variety of settings.	Focus is on *what* to learn—facts, information.
Personalized Learning	
Children add to lessons with their own stories related to the topics at hand.	Children adhere to answering questions and completing assignments given in texts and workbooks without personal elaboration.
Ability	
Individual differences are attributed to children's prior experiences.	Teacher believes individuals differ because of innate ability.
Errors in Performance	
Errors are seen as learning opportunities.	Errors are marked wrong and feedback is given child on how to correct them.
Errors reflect child's perception, which teachers try to understand.	

Learning task is messy, requiring child to "figure" out how to achieve good performance.	Learning task is broken down by teacher into simple steps for the parts that make up the task.

Participation

There are multiple opportunities for children to participate in group discussions, practice and application of newly taught whole class lessons, paired activities, games and social activities.	Children learn to attend to the teacher, follow instructions, and engage in guided concepts.

Collaboration

Children help each other, each one contributing to a common goal.	Each child does own work. Children compare their levels of performance.

Authority

Children judge their own work, prepare alternative solutions, and seek evidence for facts presented.	Teacher judges and scores child's work. Standard rubrics are used in assigning grades.

Assessment

Children have many ways to show what they know—drawing, acting, writing, building, and so on.	Both standardized tests and teacher-made tests show what child has learned.

Parent/Teacher Conference

Teacher listens to parents' concerns. Teacher acts on home-centered information as way to support both parent and child.	Teacher controls the conference, apprehensive about parents who know too much about education and schooling.
Child participates in the conference.	Child is exempted from parent-teacher conference.

Understanding Personality and Behavioral Characteristics of Gifted Children

I love to hear stories about gifted children showing their uniqueness. These encapsulated memories fill my mind with wonder and fascination, amuse me, and warm my heart. Let me share a few:

- ❑ Jacob at nine months calls the flowers in his garden bougainvilleas.
- ❑ Camden at 18 months can sing and perform the alphabet song.
- ❑ David at 20 months can name and categorize every kind of car by manufacturer.
- ❑ Matt at barely two years can put together a 64-piece puzzle.
- ❑ Jake at three is trying to understand black holes in outer space.
- ❑ Mary Katherine and Alexandra, four-year-old fraternal twins, enjoy explaining the digestive system and other aspects of the

human body with each other, their mother, and anyone else who will listen to them.

❑ Millin at seven gives a piano recital of Rachmaninoff.

❑ Dulcinee at eight performs violin in Carnegie Hall.

I can't hear enough stories like these, but we all know there are "other" moments . . . less amazing and more challenging.

You already know in your heart that your child is out of the ordinary. A standardized IQ test will show you exactly *how* gifted your child really is. As already discussed, if the score is 132, then your child is in the top 98 percentile of all children. Any score above 132 qualifies your child for gifted services through the public schools. A score of 145 or above is in the highly gifted range and the top 99 percentile of all children. The profoundly gifted (or wizard) category is a score of 160 or above, which always calls for acceleration.

You will need to discuss your child's score or singular talent with professionals in education and psychology, as well as a professional in your child's particular area of talent, to really understand what giftedness or talent means pertaining to your child. Reading about giftedness is critical. It is likewise essential to have the support of family and friends who want to understand what you are going through and who will help you make a plan for your child's educational future.

You want to learn everything about your child's educational options (see Chapter 3). With the help of your spouse or significant other, you will make the best decisions possible about your child's education and schooling. And you will prepare yourself to re-evaluate how the school and other enrichment activities you select fit your child's developmental needs on a reasonably regular basis. You have learned from Chapter 3 that there is no perfect school situation for a gifted child.

You ultimately face your most difficult problem—dealing with your little genius on a moment-to-moment, day-to-day basis. There are countless exhilarating experiences juxtaposed with overwhelming emotional distress. Most likely, you spend countless nights wondering, "What will help me get through my child's super-energized growing up years?" (By the way, I still sometimes wonder about my adult gifted children, "How will I help my son or daughter get through their less frequent but really troubling times and issues?")

Of course, all parents face the serious dilemma of how to navigate their son's or daughter's journey through childhood and adolescence. The difference for you as the parent of a gifted child is that you face the supercharged challenges with your children with less information, understanding, and guidance than parents of typical children. Parents of typical children can read books or talk to their relatives and neighbors who have children with developmental concerns that are very similar. Parents of gifted children, in a manner of speaking, are left out in the cold with just a limited number of people to talk with who will be supportive in helping them solve their everyday challenging problems. Finding a community support group for parents of the gifted can be very helpful for everyday issues, and can provide insight into to your own anxiety about raising a gifted child.

Developmental Understanding Is Invaluable

You'll find it tremendously helpful to understand what it means developmentally to have a gifted child. It is essential to know what makes very bright children so intense, so curious, and so emotional. Gifted children are more than little brainiacs, wizards, or prodigies! Gifted children are as highly sensitive in an emotional sense as they are smart in their intellectual capacity. The brighter the child the more sensitive he or she will be to others and to environmental stimulation.

Let's start our developmental understanding at birth. Very smart infants are more alert than typical infants. The attachment or the bond they form with their mother and father is highly charged and intense. Very bright babies are often highly energetic, curious, action-oriented, even rambunctious. Very, very early in life they kick, cry, move about, and start vocalizations. In general, although not in every instance, gifted children talk early, putting words together as early as nine months. Some are early walkers.

These precocious babies are more sensitive and perceptive than typical children. Their sensitivity elicits more intense responses from parents, grandparents, siblings, and other caretakers. Gifted infants, toddlers, and preschoolers need more attention and activity, as they often seem to be tireless. From birth onward, very bright babies are high maintenance.

Mothers and fathers who are appropriately attentive to their growing babies develop unique ways of interacting with them that are emotionally comforting and also stimulating to their young and curious minds. Indeed, gifted children generally start their lives in the fast lane, moving more quickly and demanding more high-quality fuel. You, in turn, have to work harder to keep up with their curiosity and strong emotions.

By toddlerdom, most gifted children are racing their parents around the house and the community. They are busy communicating through words and actions with mom and dad and anyone else who will listen to them at the grocery store, park, shopping mall, zoo, museum, airport, restaurants, theme parks, and so on. Onlookers and caretakers are often shocked to hear their vocabulary and get a sense of their smartness. At first glance, the gifted child is perceived as astonishingly precocious. They also are very perceptive; these bright youngsters have learned to get what they want from their parents, grandparents, aunts, uncles, and others who interact and spend time with them. More often than not, and quite naturally, these children have become used to a lot of attention from others. And they have an amazing ability to concentrate on activities that interest them.

Smart kids will sit and play with blocks, action figures, or the computer for hours. They can remember verbatim everything that is said to them or that they have heard from movies or television. Their memory can be unnerving. The downside to this ability to concentrate and remember is that their anger or frustration can lead them to have serious tantrums when they are unhappy. Their temper tantrums are equally unnerving and intense.

In early childhood, gifted children stand apart because of their capacity to focus on activities that they want to participate in at preschool or at home. They are incredibly focused and motivated. Equally remarkable is their emotional intensity. Often, they have serious separation anxiety from their parents because of their heightened sensitivity to new people and situations. Their imagination about what can backfire when mom leaves them alone is intense. As young children, they need a consistent routine structure in order to contain their anxiety. When there are family problems, such as financial pressures, illness, or divorce, very bright children will react strongly, feeling very fearful and insecure. They let everyone know about their unhappiness in one way or another. Some gifted children won't stop talking about their anger or pain. Others will clam up and withdraw. Young gifted children are not calm. They are temperamental and can be high strung.

A strong and supportive family structure that provides realistic expectations and consequences is most beneficial to the gifted child's development, because characteristic behaviors that are unique to the gifted evolve from the earliest moments of their life. The emotional attachments in the family that develop are played out through countless different types of interactions and are crucial to the foundation of the child's sense of self. Whereas underresponding to or neglecting a gifted child can stifle the child's overall emotional and cognitive development, overreacting to and overstimulating a gifted child creates an entitled emotional tyrant who will have problems adjusting to peers and making realistic life decisions. If you strive for a balanced approach to child rearing—not too much attention and not too little attention, you will face the rewards and difficulties of your child's development more realistically and effectively.

You will find yourself in a continued struggle to balance your child's needs for attention and stimulation with your own sanity. It is essential that you understand and deal with certain unique personality characteristics and behavioral patterns that go along with distinctive strong intellectual and emotional capacities. You cannot wish away your children's intellectual and emotional intensity. The mixture of what is genetically transmitted with the quality of the parent–child interaction will be the foundation of the child's personality structure.

Unique Behavioral Characteristics of Gifted Children

You have to accept what is unique in your gifted child. Understanding and reacting appropriately to your child's unique personality development is crucial. Knowing what you are up against definitely gives you an advantage. The following characteristics delineate the behavioral profile of a child who is either intellectually gifted or talented.

An Early and Enduring Passion for Communication

> *"My twins were talking to each other by six months. They were singing to each other and to me by their first Thanksgiving."*
>
> *—Isabella*

A bright baby uses language earlier than a typical baby. Often, very bright children talk early and are able to put words together in a meaningful way. They are able to teach themselves the alphabet, numbers, counting, and how to spell. These extremely alert babies turn into toddlers who have remarkable memories, which they use to understand what is predictable about their world and to shock their parents and relatives.

Bright youngsters can carry on adult-level conversations. I remember once having an adult conversation with my own two-year-old son in a restaurant. We were talking about the reasons we were moving to a new house. The people sitting next to me thought that I was talking to myself. They came over to see if they could "help" me. When they saw I was talking to my young child, they were extremely surprised. They quickly apologized for interrupting us. Fortunately, I continued our conversation and did not make my son feel self-conscious.

Countless times I have had serious conversations with four-year-olds who come to see me for school evaluations. Gifted three-year-olds talk about what they like to do at school as if they were six or seven. I remember an adorable little girl whose mother brought her for a school evaluation. She told me that she knew how to unbalance, manipulate, or upset her mother to get her way. In her words, "My mom gets upset when I get angry at her. If I want to get my way, I just have to get angry." I was truly shocked by her insightfulness, by how easy it was for her to predict her mother's reaction and make a plan to get her own way.

As bright children get older, they develop their passion for communication, which is usually at least two to five years more advanced than is developmentally predictable. While young, they are continually asking questions about everything. Older children demonstrate their curiosity and communication strengths by asking serious questions about people they observe or about their world. For example, they might be concerned with physical, political, educational, and moral issues. They might ask with great curiosity and in a nonhostile manner, "Why is that person so fat?" or "Why is there war?" or "What should we do about homeless people?"

Common Parental Concern: Is My Child's Verbal Ability Normal?

Parents are often amazed at their smart child's capacity to use language and his or her interest in communicating. And still, and almost in the same moment, parents seem to doubt what they hear. Or they may think, or say, "This is just 'so cute' that our baby is speaking so beautifully," as if to diminish the verbal strengths of their child.

Early use of language is usually your first clue that your child is gifted. I think parents know when their child's use of language is well above normal; they know their child is indeed advanced. Their questions about advanced language skills seem to be an attempt to get more understanding of how their child is really different from the typical child. In addition, these concerns are the parents' first awareness of, and usually their first anxiety, about the fact that their child is gifted.

Common Reactions Parents Have to Their Child's Precocious Use of Language

"Good Enough" Reaction

"It is so exciting and wonderful to have a child who can talk to me and wants to communicate."

This response supports and promotes pride, self-esteem, and bonding between parent and child.

Undermining Reactions

"Wow! I think we have a little genius here. Let's parade him around and show him off to all of the neighbors and relatives. Let's get him an audience."

This response undermines the development of the child's sense of self, because it makes the child's performance more important than the child's feelings and thoughts and it is a subtle form of exploitation.

> "Let's just ignore our child. He is just too strange. We never wanted to have a genius."

The child's potential is totally ignored. This is a totally disastrous parental attitude.

A Remarkable Capacity for Concentration

> *"My son has an unbelievable ability to focus and concentrate. You can see the wheels turning in his head, and the thorough contemplation of the possibilities, inputs, and likely outcomes."*   —Tony

Bright babies, toddlers, and growing children are able to concentrate for long periods of time. They become fascinated with an object, game, or a toy and seem to lose interest in everything around them. Through playing, their powers of concentration grow and develop into interests that eventually shape their identity in adolescence and into adulthood. Concentration—the positive aspect of perfectionism—becomes a determining influence of their personality and intellectual strength.

Common Parental Concern: Should I Take Away the Thomas the Train Set or Turn the Computer Off?

Sometimes parents ask this question with amusement and pride in their face. Sometimes parents are dead serious. The answer to the question of when is enough *enough* has to be based on practicalities. This means that if time and place permits, let your baby, toddler, or school-age child play as long as he or she wants with something that is special and compelling or fascinating. However, children need to understand that it is not always possible to get their own way. You need to explain to your small child *when* it will be a good time and place to play. You will need to explain this again and again to your school-age child, and then all over again when they are adolescents.

In most homes, playing in the playroom, family room, porch, or backyard is the right place, when mom is not too busy to supervise. The wrong place or time to play is when mom or dad needs to get something done. For example, dinnertime is not playtime. Errand time is not playtime. Homework time is not playtime.

It is critical that you allow your child time to play, as well as set limits for when playtime is not possible. With older children, the same rules apply. Gifted children are strong willed and self-centered. They need to learn to respect authority and follow the house rules. To allow children free reign is to invite chaos in your home and life.

Common Reactions Parents Have to the Overfocused Child

Your best reaction is based on your understanding that your child's concentration is a part of her personality. In this context, you will be able to set appropriate limits.

"Good-Enough" Reaction

> "Now is a good time for you to play with your computer. In half an hour we will be having dinner and you will need to turn the computer off."

This response affirms the child's interests as well as putting their interest into the perspective of family life.

Undermining Reaction

> "Stop this now. I have told you over and over again to turn off the computer. You are a bad listener."

This reaction is humiliating and guilt-inducing. It is never a good idea to scream at your child. Screaming lets your child know that you are out of control, and sends the message that it is okay for your child to get out of control and scream as well.

Persistence in Mastering a Task

> *"Once my child gets started on understanding something, she becomes obsessed with its completion. When she decided at age five that she wanted to understand how the human body works, I could not quell her curiosity. First she dissected a frog and then a fetal pig. Then I had to call it quits in trying to satisfy her curiosity."* —Carolyn

Building on their powers of concentration, gifted children use persistence to understand and master a task. At first, the toddler and then the preschooler puts blocks together, learns the alphabet, and develops collections of cars, trucks, or whatever items fascinate them. Later, this same child wants to understand the basics of more complicated tasks and processes. Whether he or she is learning to play the piano, studying a foreign language, dissecting a frog, studying astronomy, or writing a play or poetry, gifted children do not give up on their mission to master the task they are curious about conquering with perfect attention to detail.

Common Parental Concern: How Much Should I Give In to My Child's Demand to Understand Everything? How Much Is Too Much?

Gifted children are unusually highly motivated, which is fascinating and remarkable. When indulged, their motivation to understand all of the details can cross the line into persistent nagging and even parental abuse. First, you need to be clear on what is appropriate to tell your child about adult issues such as sexuality, drugs, and interpersonal relationships. Next, you need to set realistic limits when it comes to your child's demanding curiosity about child-appropriate issues.

Indeed, intense curiosity can be daunting to parents of highly gifted children, who are expected to know the answers to every question they are asked. When your child is young, you will have to teach your little "bottomless pit of questions" how to find some of the answers on his or her own. As early as possible, children can learn to use the dictionary, the encyclopedia, or even the Internet. These skills are critical to their intellectual development and to your sanity.

If you devote your life to answering every question your child asks, you will surely raise an emotional tyrant who does not understand when to respect another person's limitations. When your child is clearly demanding ridiculous amounts of attention, you should suspect that you are overextending yourself and making your child too important.

Common Reaction of Parents to the Persistent Quest for Knowledge

"Good Enough" Reaction

"I am delighted that you are interested in understanding why there are black holes in space! Usually the preschool teacher does not cover outer space. When we have extra time, we can go to the library and get a book about the solar system."

This response encourages the child but also sets realistic limits on what a mother or father can do. By modeling good judgment, you are teaching your child that using good judgment is important.

Undermining Reactions

"Why can't you ask normal questions like other children?"

This response indicates that you are lazy. It makes your child feel like a misfit. You don't want to do this to your child's developing sense of self.

> "I'm not going to drop everything I am doing to explain black holes to you! I'm not going to answer any more of your questions!"

This response tells your child that you are not interested enough to help. It makes the child feel foolish and unimportant. It might even make the child feel guilty for being curious.

Emotional Intensity

> *"My son saturates himself with each feeling. He experiences life through a magnifying glass, strengthening himself with every feeling. Even life's nuances are grand and clear. Sometimes you think he's just being overly sensitive, but he truly is affected times ten in all things."*
>   —Tony

> *"At three he would cry, no, wail at an aria in* Le Nozze di Figaro, *begging me to turn it off because it was 'too beautiful,' and he couldn't take it."*
>   —Mary

> *"At moments like these, it's an interesting line we parents must walk in understanding and nurturing, yet instilling a balance they'll need to function well in society, without discounting their sincerest emotions."*
>   —Julia

> *"His depth of feelings are so profound that I worry that other kids his age won't understand his passion and intensity and the other children will tease him. His feelings are genuine and I want him to know that it is okay to express his feelings. I worry about other people thinking he is overemotional."*
>   —Cynthia

Gifted children have unique personality and behavioral characteristics, which are rooted in a deep emotional intensity. A gifted child's emotional intensity is commensurate with or equal to his or her intellectual strengths. Indeed, the capacity for deep and complex thought is also manifested in a complicated and intense emotional life.

Emotional complexity can be seen in the vast range of emotions that very bright children experience about a single event. For example, a gifted five-year-old child sees a homeless person sitting by the side of the local market. She asks her mom, "What is wrong with that person?" (an expression of curiosity) "Can we give her some money?" (an expression of her concern) "What will happen to her tonight when it gets cold?" (an expression of fear) "Can she live with us, mom?" (an expression of compassion and generosity) Parents and teachers who work with giftedness are familiar with these types of complicated reactions.

Emotional intensity is a *vivid* way of experiencing life. This intensity fuels joy in life, passion for learning, the expression of talent, and the drive to excel at a task or project. The gifted child expresses emotional intensity in many different ways. Consider the following examples:

- ❏ *Moodiness—strong positive and negative emotions that change in a short period of time about people.* "I love you mommy, you are the best." Moments later: "I hate you mommy, you ruined my life."

- ❏ *Body sensations such as stomachaches or headaches or nausea, which are symptoms of fearful feelings.* "I can't go to school today; I have a horrible stomachache."

- ❏ *Timidity or shyness as an expression of strong feelings of inhibition.* "I can't go outside and play with the other children; it's too scary."

- ❏ *Strong emotional memories of past experiences that are relived when they are remembered.* An adopted five-year-old starts to cry when remembering the time she met her natural mother.

- ❏ *Fears, anxiety, or guilt about mistakes that may happen.* "I don't think I did my homework right. The teacher will be angry with me."

❑ *Strong empathy for others.* "Mom, a girl in the class lost her dog and she is so sad. Can we find her another dog?"

❑ *Self-criticism and feelings of inadequacy and worthlessness that can crop up easily and be felt with the same strength as seen in adults.* "It's all my fault that Dad isn't coming home. I guess his work is more important than me."

Emotional intensity can be frightening or painful to a child if ignored or criticized. You need to accept and then deal with the behavioral manifestations of these profound feelings. If handled appropriately, strong feelings inspire talent, passion, and genius. If ignored, strong feelings can turn into frustration, sadness, depression, and acting-out behavior with drugs, sexuality, and general alienation from society.

Common Parental Concern: Why Is My Child So Emotional? Is There Anything I Can Do About It?

Gifted children are as emotional as they are smart. Some researchers suggest that the child's level of emotionality is directly related to their IQ score. A child with a 145 IQ is very emotional or sensitive but less emotional or excitable than a child with an IQ of 170. There is no way to get around this reality! You need to know and accept that your child's emotionality is not your fault, and that it is not a sign of psychological conflicts or disturbance.

Although some researchers believe that gifted children have more psychiatric disorders than normal children, other researchers argue the opposite point of view. Gifted children are no more vulnerable to depression and anxiety than normal children. There is no proof one way or the other. There is just concern!

You need to accept that your child is very sensitive and intense. Although there will be times when your child is very logical and calm, the emotional side may easily and quickly take over. One parent summed the issue up: "My husband and I used to wonder at the start of each day who will emerge from the bedroom—our daughter or her evil twin. Really, though, the surprise was on more of a moment-to-moment basis. Would it be the intellectual child or the emotional one?"

When I consult with gifted children and adolescents who are very prone to mood swings, I try to pay attention to their emotions as well as their thoughtfulness. I give importance to both and allow the child to come to his/her own conclusions. I always advise parents to let their children learn to respect their own feelings and thoughts. However, this does not mean that smart children can act in any way that they want to. For example, your child may be angry, but that does not mean that he or she can tear up the kitchen.

I believe that if you label children as too emotional or too smart, they will come to believe their label. This typing or labeling of "too emotional" leads children to self-doubt and confusion. Parents who delight in their child's emotional intensity, but do not let this intensity run their lives, are the most effective.

Common Reaction to Emotional Outbursts

Let's say your daughter slams the phone down after a fight with her best friend and starts bawling. You may feel like saying to her, "This is not the end of the world." There are better alternatives.

"Good Enough" Reaction

> "I can see that you are disappointed with your best friend. When you feel like talking about what happened between the two of you, I will be eager to listen."

By responding with empathy, you allow your child to experience and process her feelings, and you are not making your child feel bad about her emotional state of mind. By describing your child's feelings, you are containing your child's feelings—letting your child know that feelings are important.

Undermining Reactions

"You need to stop overreacting like this."

"I am really tired of your overinvolvement with your friends."

"Your behavior is exhausting me and making me sick."

These reactions make your child feel guilty about her feelings, which will surely intensify these feelings and make the whole situation much worse. By being critical, you are pushing your child away from confiding in you. Gifted children are smart enough to find people who will take them seriously. Unfortunately, not everyone will give your child good advice.

Perfectionism

"My son started playing the piano at 5. If he could not play all of his music perfectly, he would cry and be very angry at himself. We had to stop his lessons for several months until he could regain his composure and concentrate on learning."   —Rachel

Perfectionism is a part of the curiosity and persistence that compels gifted children to understand a situation, task, or interaction. Because perfectionism is so central to the bright child's core self or identity, perfectionism can become a serious problem if it spirals out of control. Gifted children need to learn to deal with their perfectionism. Specifically, they need to learn that they will not be able to do everything perfectly. This is a hard lesson to teach your smart child. Your success as a teacher will be directly related to your convictions about perfectionism and your ability to make mistakes yourself.

Common Parental Concern: Why Is My Child Such a Perfectionist? Did I Create This Monster?

Getting your child's perfectionist tendencies under control is a very important parental task for parents. Blaming yourself for your child's need to do everything right is not the answer. Instead, develop a strategy for dealing with your son's or daughter's perfectionism. Re-read Chapter 2 and use the suggestions to find a plan that works for you and your child.

Common Reactions to Perfectionism

Your six-year-old son has spent two hours on his homework. You think to yourself that your child is really obsessed. But don't bring this up.

"Good Enough" Reaction

"I can see that you are disappointed that you don't have time to complete your work perfectly. What you have done is good enough. You will have more time tomorrow."

By saying this you put the entire problem with perfectionism into perspective.

Undermining Reaction

"You are becoming a freak about completing this homework! You are a monster! I should have your head examined. Your behavior is going to give me a nervous breakdown."

This is a guilt-inducing and out-of-control reaction. As the adult, you need to be in charge of developing your child's self-esteem—not destroying it.

Anxiety over Separation and New Situations

"I told the kindergarten teacher that my son looked upset that I was leaving him all alone on the first day of school. I explained to her that I stayed with him the first couple of weeks at preschool to help him with his separation anxiety. The teacher was very firm with me.

She said, 'He will stop crying; you should leave. All of the children
cry for two or three minutes when their mothers leave them.

   "When I returned three hours later, the teacher was very happy
to see me. She said, 'Your son cried for almost three hours. Now he is
calm and playing with the other kids.'"   —Leslie

Because gifted children are emotionally intense and have a heightened sensitivity to others, they can imagine a lot of negative possibilities. They often suffer from anxiety in new situations. This
might include a new school, a new babysitter, a vacation, or even
a trip to a theme park.

   The best way to deal with this anticipatory anxiety is to prepare
your child for the new experience he or she is about to experience. Do
not underestimate their capacity to imagine what might go wrong.
In turn, prepare yourself for their genuine happiness and pride when
they master the new situation. You might wonder why they are so
dramatic. How real are their fears if they recover so easily?

Common Parental Concern: When Will Their Anxiety Subside or Diminish?

With gifted children, the reduction of their anxiety is usually tran-
sient, as well as dependent on the situation they are facing. The more
personally stressful the situation for the child, the more intense their
anxiety. Only with time will you understand the meaning of what
is so difficult for them.

   Let me underline that your son or daughter's anxiety about a
new situation is different than your anxiety. For example, I worked
on a school evaluation of a eight-year-old who had just performed
in Carnegie Hall. Before I met with Dulcinee, I was sure that her parents had pushed her into this performance. I was anticipating how
anxiety-provoking this concert must have been for her. When I was
talking with Dulcinee, however, I learned that she loved performing

and looked forward to every concert she was asked to participate in. She told me that playing the violin in Carnegie Hall was "fun." Her trip to New York City was only difficult when she went shopping for new school clothes.

Another example points out that parents can't and don't always understand what is making their son or daughter so anxious. Janice and Matt are devoted parents of ten-year-old David, who can be anxious at school or at home. His blinking eyes reveal the light of his inner turmoil. Both parents try to understand their son's issues. School work, the teacher connection, and peer pressure are possibilities. There is no clear-cut answer. Only with time does David's anxiety retreat. His parents have to accept that they are not always sure about what is bothering him. Finally, and in some magical way, the unknown troublesome issues provoke less anxiety for this now-teenager and the eye-blinking behavior stops.

Common Reactions to Intense Separation Anxiety

Let's say your child is afraid to attend a birthday party.

"Good Enough" Reaction

"I can see that you are very anxious about attending your friend's party. What are you most concerned about?"

This reaction accepts the child's feelings, as well as letting the child figure out how to solve the problem. You are not giving in to your child's fear that he or she cannot manage anxiety. And you are not ignoring the child's feelings.

Undermining Reactions

"Everything will be all right. You are just overreacting."

"I don't know why you are such a baby. Why can't you just enjoy yourself like the other kids? Your anxiety is going to lead me to an early grave."

These reactions are critical, humiliating, and guilt-inducing. They make your child feel like a baby who can't control his or her feelings. In addition, they make your child feel alienated from you.

A Strong Inclination Toward Introspection and Insight

> *"My son Benny is so upset with himself for having problems with his math homework. He blames himself and calls himself stupid. I try to explain to him that he will get better with practice. This does not help. When Ben is really upset he tells me that he wishes he had not been born."*
> —Jessica

A hallmark of a child's giftedness can be seen in their capacity to look inward using insight to try and understand what is happening outside his or her world. I know both from personal and professional experiences that gifted children are notorious for sizing up a situation and thinking that they caused the problem. I can only speculate on why gifted children are so quick to blame themselves for unfortunate circumstances. I believe it might be their curiosity and need to solve a problem or find resolution to something that is bothering them. You should always explain to your children that they are not at fault for things they did not do.

Another aspect of introspection is often seen when gifted children develop imaginary friends.

Common Parental Concern: Why Is My Child So Depressed at Such an Early Age?

Some parents are seriously concerned that the introspection and the insight of the gifted child is abnormal and based on childhood depression. Others are concerned that their child is strange, different, or atypical because of an interest and capacity to look at psychological motivation.

My response to these concerns is to reassure parents that their children are *not* seriously off balance. My experience and understanding suggest that introspection and insight are normal for gifted children. Parents should talk openly with their children about serious adult issues that they bring up and try to be reassuring in order to quell their child's worry and deal with their feelings of loneliness.

Common Reactions to a Child's Insightful Introspection

Your five-year-old tells you that she knows she is smarter than the other kids at school and feels bad about herself that she does not fit in with the popular crowd.

"Good Enough" Reaction

> "I'm glad you were able to trust me enough to share your thoughts and feelings with me about how you feel about being smart."

This response mirrors the child's feelings and contains them. The child can then accept that her feelings are normal and acceptable to you. This encourages a deeper attachment with your child.

Undermining Reactions

> "There you go having those weird thoughts about being smarter than everyone at school." "I know that you are the smartest kid at school. I've told you so a million times."

These reactions disregard the child's feelings. They serve to humiliate the child and undermine the development of self-esteem.

Asynchronous Development—Learning Highs and Lows

"Yes! Rachelle feels she should excel at everything so she gets really frustrated when she doesn't or something is difficult for her. She avoids putting herself in a situation where she knows she won't do well. She will try new things and has astounding determination if she wants to master something."   —Sheila

"Matt can do very complicated math with his calculator, but he has a very hard time with simple addition. His vocabulary is astonishing, but his handwriting is atrocious."   Diana

Gifted children pick up most learning tasks very quickly. But they are not good at everything. Understandably, they are more comfortable with what comes easily to them. They have difficulty when they have to struggle, as they are not familiar with this experience. Parents can and do become frustrated with their child's uneven learning capacities. When you have realistic expectations for your child's learning potential, your effectiveness as a parent will increase. *Asynchronous development* is the term used by some gifted educators to explain the phenomena.

Young gifted children are not immediately aware that they learn differently from the other children. Gradually they realize that they are quicker and more energetic than their peers when it comes to learning. As youngsters, they are just familiar with their own swift pace, which is very engaging for them. In turn, smart children don't know how to learn what does *not* come to them instantaneously. They must be taught how to learn material that is difficult for them. For example, handwriting is a common problem. You need to set small, achievable goals that will lead to your child's eventual mastery. While you are waiting patiently for your child to learn a difficult task, talk with your child about learning challenges.

Be patient. This is your best option. And remember, as gifted children get older they start to understand that they learn differently than other children. They become aware of their own quickness in certain areas and difficulties in other areas. This self-awareness helps them to learn how to work on the areas that are more difficult for them.

Common Parental Concern: Why Is My Child So Smart and Then So Dense? Is My Child Really Gifted?

This is a typical and normal refrain, which is based on your own frustration with your son or daughter. Try to step back from these negative feelings. Try not to act on your anger. (I know this is very difficult advice to follow.) Getting angry that your child is having difficulties will only make a bad situation worse. Remember, your child is very sensitive and is probably very upset about doing poorly. Your child may feel like he or she is disappointing you.

Your first step is to ask calmly, "Can I help you with (whatever the problem may be)?" Or, for example, "Do you need tutoring?" Try to be positive. You might say, "Nobody is good at everything. With time and practice, you will get better!"

This problem crops up regularly. For example, Deena was a warm and adorable five-year-old who seemed to have trouble learning to read. Her older brother, Frank, a second grader, had been an avid reader even as a preschooler. The house was filled with all types of books for every age and stage of life. Mom and Dad were not concerned that Deena was incapable of learning to read. Her parents knew intuitively that negative thinking would not help. Her mom believed that when she was ready, Deena would read. She was tutored in first grade because the classroom teacher made this suggestion. Deena liked being tutored, but she didn't learn to read. On her own she started reading at age seven, and then she read perfectly!

Common Reactions to Asynchronous Development

Avoid the temptation to communicate hysteria or guilt.

"Good Enough" Reaction

"I see that you are having problems in certain subjects at school. I am going to find someone to help you with the area that is a challenge for you."

This reaction teaches your child coping skills. It shows that you don't expect perfection. It allows your child to relax when he or she is not the best student.

Undermining Reactions

"I can't believe you are gifted. You are really being stupid."

"How many times do we have to go over this material?"

"Why can't you be more like your brother?"

These reactions lower your child's self-esteem. They contribute to the underachievement syndrome; they are humiliating. This negative reaction should be avoided no matter what.

Issues with Underachievement or Overachievement

"My son loves going to school. The school has accelerated him from grade one to grade three. He is so happy with all of the extra work."

—Jonathan

"My daughter hates to go to junior school. Even though she is extremely bright, she is failing her important classes."   —Mark

Talent or achievement that is way above average is a natural manifestation of giftedness. Overachievement, pride in productivity, or underachievement in an area of strength can all reflect the child's overall self-concept. Overachievement can be an early and easy way to obtain approval from parents and teachers. Achieving for others as a way of showing off can be overdone and counterproductive because it is not derived from the "true self." Underachievement is an expression of anger and frustration at the school or at the family. Underachievement may signal to parents and teachers that the gifted child is bored and may be depressed. Clearly, gifted children who set their own pace based on their own curiosity or inclinations are better off.

Common Parental Concerns: What Can I Do to Help My Child Work Up to His/Her Potential? Am I Pushing Too Hard?

Both of these questions can be perplexing. Getting a sense of your child's academic strengths and other talents is crucial. Parents who ask teachers or tutors for help and who work with their child's school and the individuals in charge of outside activities are usually the most successful.

You will need to be your child's advocate, not the child's talent agent or producer. Look inside yourself for the answer. "Does my daughter love to give piano concerts or does she do it to make me happy?" "Why is my child underachieving? Is it a way to tell me he is unhappy?" (See Chapter 6.)

Common Reactions to Achievement Issues and Remarkable Talent

Your child is the star of the team that goes to a championship spelling bee. She is very nervous.

"Good Enough" Reaction

"This is an important learning experience for you. It doesn't matter if you win or lose, you will learn something about the other students and about competition."

This reaction does not pressure your child and puts competition into proper perspective.

Undermining Reaction

"You better practice those spelling charts. The entire family is coming to the spelling bee and I don't want you to lose."

This reaction pressures your child and provides her with an externalizing motivation that ultimately creates burnout. It also teaches your child that winning is more important than how you play the game.

Socialization Problems

"My daughter only hangs out with the smart girls at school. She never goes to a dance or a football game."   —Sharon

"My husband and I are having problems with our marriage and our son is acting very regressed at school."   —Sara

"My son has friends that are a lot older than he is."   —Leslie

"My daughter is very anxious when she is placed in a new peer group at school."   —Charles

Gifted children are very sensitive and intuitive. They can form wonderful, deep friendships. Normal socialization issues are usually related to the extreme difference between the interests of typical children and gifted children. Because gifted children are highly curious, they are often seen as eggheads, nerds, or brainiacs by other nongifted peers. Parents and teachers really need to make special efforts to make very smart children feel like they are a part of the school community. It is very common for smart children to feel like outsiders and freaks. Sometimes very bright children dumb themselves down to fit into the "in" crowd.

There is no "normal" way for gifted children to adjust to their peer age group. Gifted children who are accelerated in kindergarten and first grade usually make the best adjustments to their social group at school. Other healthy adjustments are related to the development of a peer group based on similar interests such as music, art, sports, theater, and so on.

Socialization can be arrested or held back if there are family problems. When the match between the child and the school is inadequate, social issues can surface. A lack of social adjustment is found in children whose talent has been pushed too hard or overemphasized at the expense of other aspects of their identity. For example, highly gifted children in dance, music, science, and so on who are overfocused in their one area of achievement or talent are usually undersocialized and can become very uncomfortable in normal day-to-day social situations. Later in life, these talented individuals often are at the mercy of husbands, talent agents, or business managers, who make their decisions for them.

The most dangerous adjustments to a social group are those based on depression and acting out with drugs and sexuality. Oftentimes gifted children who have been ignored by their parents and have no outlet for their talents turn against themselves by getting involved with potentially self-destructive and deadly behavior.

Common Parental Concern: Will My Gifted Child Have an Overinflated Sense of Self if My Child Is Always Being Described as Gifted?

This is a tricky question, and parents are often looking for different types of answers. Of course, some parents, who are living through their children's accomplishments *do* want their children to have an overinflated sense of themselves. With this disclaimer in mind, my general answer to this question is no. If children are reared with love and discipline and taught to respect their gifts as well as those of others, they will not grow up to be conceited or self-possessed.

Common Reactions to Socialization Issues Involving Shyness

Your child is a musical prodigy who loves performing. You can see that he feels awkward in social situations. Instead of pointing his fearfulness out, it is better just to encourage him to interact with others.

"Good Enough" Reaction

"I'm so pleased that you are making friends at your music class."

This reaction allows your child to develop his musical talent and his self-esteem.

Undermining Reaction

"You are such a talented musician, I don't understand why you are so uncomfortable when you have to talk to people after the performance."

This response praises musical talent but humiliates your child in terms of social skills and makes him feel ashamed of himself.

Ability to Act Older Than They Feel

"My daughter is only seven years old but she talks to me about very personal issues as if she were an adult. Yesterday she and I spoke about the loss of one of my dear friends. She was very compassionate and seemed to understand what the loss meant to me."   —Marjorie

Gifted children act older than their actual chronological age. Their vocabulary, understanding, and capacity to reason are more advanced than nongifted children. They are often more comfortable with adults or older children who are at their intellectual level. Don't get confused when your child talks as if he or she has great maturity and then acts like a much younger child. You need to accept that emotional growth and development are not always as advanced as your child's capacity to think about an issue.

Be aware that a gifted child may be able to talk beautifully and logically about the birth of a new brother, the death of a beloved grandmother, or the move to a new city. When emotionally confronted with the new baby, the funeral, or the actual relocation, however, the child might act like a much younger person. You have to be careful not to penalize your child for acting his or her age.

In addition, although gifted children are very logical, their judgment will lag behind their reasoning capacity. Smart individuals learn to use good judgment through their experiences.

Common Parental Concern: How Do I Cope with My Child's Grown-Up Behavior that Instantly Turns into Age-Appropriate Behavior?

You have to learn to switch gears quickly. Remember that they are only children; you are the adult. Sometimes it is helpful to think about what situations are difficult for your child and to anticipate the possibility of a change in state of mind.

Common Reactions to Changing States of Mind

"Good Enough" Reaction

> "I can see that you were excited about attending the ballet. I can really understand how hard it is for you to be still for such a long time. It's okay with me if you want to take a break and go outside."

This response allows the child to strive to be grown up but also allows her to be a child.

Undermining Reaction

"You told me you wanted to attend this ballet for months. You are going to sit still until it is over, no matter what!"

This is a sure-fire way to punish and alienate your child just for being a kid and to turn her off to higher types of learning.

Thinking They Can Outsmart Their Parents and Make Up Their Own Rules

"I am much smarter than my parents."

—Just about every gifted child or adolescent kid that I have spoken with over my lifetime

Most gifted children and teenagers think that they are more intelligent than their parents and very capable of outsmarting them. Most are logical thinkers who pay good attention to detail. Because they enjoy independent thinking and creative problem solving, they also like to make up their own rules. Parents and teachers need to set clear boundaries about which rules need to be followed always and no matter what. Sometimes children can make up the rules, when safety issues are not involved and there is a purpose or reason for why they are calling the shots.

Common Parental Concern: How Do I Teach My Child to Listen to Me and Other Authority Figures?

This is a very common problem that has stymied many gifted parents of gifted children. You are more likely to be successful if you try to establish rules that are reasonable and that can be followed. Parents who are too strict will find their children rebelling. Parents who are too flexible and open-minded about setting limits tend to have demanding and insecure children who have problems following the rules.

Common Problems of Children Who Think They Are Smarter Than Adults

Your child says something like, "You know I am smarter than you are, Mom. I can stay up and work on my computer all night."

"Good Enough" Reaction

"I realize you are very talented with your computer, but you still need to get your rest."

This response acknowledges the child's curiosity and passions as well as realistic parental concerns.

Undermining Reaction

"You are not as smart as you think. I am the boss in this house. And don't you forget it!"

This response sets up power struggles between parent and child as well as undermining the child's self-esteem.

Wishy-Washy Reaction

"Well, you know the rules about bedtime. But this time I will let you stay up for an extra hour as a compromise. What do you say?"

Meeting the Challenge of Raising a Gifted Child

Gifted children have a unique pattern of personality development and unusual behavioral characteristics, which have been described in this chapter. The intensity and challenge of raising these children is undeniable. You will be more effective if you are able to understand and respond to your smart child's idiosyncratic behavior. Develop realistic rules and expectations for your curious and highly sensitive children and you will find that family life moves along more calmly. Become your child's advocate, not business manager, and you will raise children of whom you can and will be proud. In turn, gifted children who are appropriately parented are more able to develop into well-adjusted and productive members of society.

Questions for you to consider:
1. What behavioral characteristics of a gifted child does my child have?
2. What is the most difficult characteristic to deal with, and why?
3. What is the most difficult characteristic for my partner to deal with, and why?
4. Are my reactions to my child's problems appropriate, or do I undermine my child's sense of self by expecting too much or too little?
5. Does my child have learning highs and lows—asynchronous development?
6. What are the most effective ways to motivate my child?
7. How does my child interact with peers?
8. Can my child follow the family and school rules? If not, why not?
9. Does my child have structured time for creative activities?
10. Does my child talk to me about his interests or passions?
11. Do I have realistic expectations for my child's school achievement?
12. Am I my child's advocate or talent agent?

Learning to Talk to Your "Know-It-All" Child

> "Sometimes it's very easy to talk with a highly gifted child. My oldest son, who is now 12, sometimes seems like another adult, he is so sensitive and insightful (not to mention the adult vocabulary he uses). In another sense, however, talking to a gifted child is difficult. Because they can seem so adult, it's easy to forget they have the emotions and the limited experience of children. You forget that they don't know about the adult world, and you have to constantly remind yourself to make sure you explain to them things that adults take for granted. Like, you can't change other people (at least not generally!) and you need to find a way to live with them. And, that elementary school won't last forever, and things will get better."
>
> Janice

All parents, and especially parents of gifted children, have to learn how to understand and talk to their children if they hope to establish a meaningful, vibrant, and long-lasting relationship with them. Talking to your gifted child in a way that can produce an open dialogue is one of your most rewarding, yet difficult, challenges.

Learning to be appropriately attentive to your child and developing an effective style of communication are necessary and worthwhile investments of your energy and time.

Communicating with a very bright child can be more difficult and draining than with a more typical child because gifted children are often emotionally intense, highly curious, deeply thoughtful, and very capable of and inclined toward argumentativeness or introspection. You need to develop specific verbal skills and strategies in order to effectively respond to your child's curiosity and to quell his or her combativeness and self-doubt. Equally important is your own emotional wherewithal, which will allow you to pay attention to, understand, and respond to your child's emotional ups and downs, perfectionism, and tendency toward obsessional thinking.

Let's look at some basic communication issues and skills.

To Whom Am I Talking?

Maybe you don't actually think about how you are going to connect with someone. You just know that in order to have a productive conversation, you need to speak the other person's language if you want to be understood. This is especially true with your child. You need to know where your child is coming from and accept where your child is developmentally. Know what matters to your child. What does your child like and dislike? Where does your child shine? Where does your child struggle? What activities and interactions will help develop self-esteem? What will undermine your child's self-worth?

Always remember that your child is different from you and your spouse, and not only because of age. Your child has experienced a different type of childhood than you did. If you are able to see your child as separate and distinct from yourself, you will find it much easier to know your child. Knowing your child as he or she is allows understanding to develop and grow. Understanding is the basis of all communication, which is what talking is all about.

You will be more effective if you keep in mind the reality that even though your gifted child may at times talk and act like an adult, he or she still is a child. You need to learn to wear different hats as you try to develop ways of relating to your child's changing states of mind from mature to childish. When your child is confused or disappointed about something, he or she may need to be comforted as a child. Oftentimes when your child is in a calm state, he or she will want to be treated like an adult, and you might decide to react on a grown-up level.

Parents of very bright kids quickly learn that their gifted children can be *know-it-alls* who like to get their own way. Sometimes they believe they *have* to get their own way, and they can and will persist against all odds. It is common for smart kids to argue every point, large or small, with their parents. Areas of conflict or discussion can include food, clothes, books, or politics, for example. How you handle these conflicts is crucial to your role as an effective parent.

What is the best approach to take when you are developing a way of communicating with your child? The first clear challenge involves recognizing what state of mind your child is in when you begin a dialogue. What is your child really asking for, and what does your child need? You, of course, should attempt to be calm and composed. Predictably and understandably, it's not always possible to maintain a calm state of mind! Which hat do you wear? Which persona do you take on? Ultimately, it is your decision how you react to your child.

- Are you the coach?
- Are you the sergeant at arms?
- Are you just mom or dad?
- Are you the untiring and unconditional support?
- Are you the tutor?

- ❑ Are you the caterer?
- ❑ Are you the car service?
- ❑ Are you the psychologist?
- ❑ Are you the Supreme Court, laying down the law?

The answer is that you are all of these to your child at one time or another.

What Is the Real Problem?

Your house is in shambles. Your older child is fighting with the younger child. The phone won't stop ringing. The dog is barking. The ant farm broke and you have ants crawling all over your house. Your husband will be home in three minutes, and he has told you in no uncertain terms that he wants his house to be quiet and dinner to be on the table for a change. You can remember a time in your life when you were in control—before your kids were born. You feel panic and don't know what to do next.

It is normal not to be sure what problem to attend to first; still, your uncertainty can be very stressful. You know you should make decisions about how to react to your highly sensitive gifted children who are totally out of control. When you are feeling panic, it will help you to remember that you do have options and solutions, even when you don't know what the real problem is. Calming everyone down will be a start, but where do you go from there?

Let's rule out surefire parental mistakes first. Often used but INEFFECTIVE solutions are as follows:

- ❑ Ignoring your child usually does not work out well for your long-term relationship.
- ❑ Screaming and yelling or being overtly aggressive is a very short-term solution to any parenting problem.

❏   Acting in a way that shames or humiliates your child will surely damage his or her self-esteem and self-confidence and drive a wedge between both of you, destroying any closeness you share.

Understanding what your child is feeling and why he or she is behaving in a certain way is your most effective starting point. If you can understand where your child is coming from, then you are accepting your child's feelings, which is basic to real communication. Learn to listen to what your child is telling you. Listening and understanding should be your first option. Let's look at four examples of how to understand your child's feelings and behavior, and then how to approach talking to your child.

HARRY AND THE POTS AND PANS: UNDERSTANDING AND TALKING TO A VERY CURIOUS TODDLER

Harry, an extremely curious 2½-year-old, is tearing up the kitchen cabinets that he can reach. You walk into the kitchen and see the mess. You immediately feel enraged and perhaps a little flabbergasted. Your darling Harry has destroyed the order in your kitchen while you were on the phone with your mother.

These thoughts and feelings run through your mind:

1. You want to scream, "STOP THIS NOW." You know in your heart that Harry is very sensitive, and that this reaction will frighten him. Besides, screaming is counterproductive because it can make your child more defiant.

2. You have talked to other mothers who let their children do whatever they want to do in the house, including drawing on the walls, to encourage their self-expression. You dismiss this nonapproach to discipline. You know that children need limits, especially Harry.

3. You remind yourself how you hated it when your mom and dad humiliated you. You decide not to shame Harry and undermine his self-esteem.

4. You may feel like you need to be in control as the parent, or as a throwback to your own childhood, when you were out of control. You realize that being in charge is very different than being in control.

Decision Point and Intervention

You decide to try to understand what is really going on in Harry's mind. This is a form of acceptance, which is the basis of communication. You empathize with Harry about his curiosity. You could say with enthusiasm, "I bet you had a really exciting time finding out what was inside my kitchen cupboards." By empathizing with your child, you are giving him the message that his feelings are important to you, and that he is, in turn, a valuable and important child. And then you need to set some limits.

Harry will sense that you respect his curiosity. He still needs to hear how you are going to set limits on his unacceptable behavior. You might say, "Mommy is going to get you a set of children's pot and pans to play with in your room and at the park. They also have a play kitchen at our 'Mommy and Me' class. It is not okay with me if you play with the adult-size pots and pans. These are for cooking only."

Harry might start to cry. Or he might say that he is sorry. Harry might get angry at you and start banging the pots on the floor in defiance. Whatever his reaction, it is important not to dismiss the child's feelings. You can say, "I understand that you are _____, but I still need to tell you that playing with my pots and pans is not okay with me."

By identifying and acknowledging your young child's feelings, you are developing his sense of self and identity, as well as understanding and accepting them. However, allowing or encouraging the inappropriate behavior is going too far. It is not a good parenting strategy to accept bad behavior, because it teaches your child that you will accept clever misbehavior. Remember, as gifted children get older there are more temptations to bend the rules with friends. If children have been taught the difference between right and wrong, and the importance of respecting authority, they will be able to adjust to the demands of their friendships, school, and their community.

You might also set up some new rules for yourself. Perhaps you need to give Harry more playtime at the park, at school, or with friends. Consider waiting until Harry goes to bed before spending time on the phone with your mother. Ask your husband to develop some special interests with Harry that include exploration.

"Good Enough" Communication

1. Identify and acknowledge your child's feelings. Tell your child in an empathic tone that you understand how he or she feels. By doing this you are accepting your child and developing his sense of self.

2. Alongside your communicated empathy for your child's feelings, set appropriate limits, which include the safety and health of your child and your family.

3. Pay attention to your child's reaction to your behavior and acknowledge your child's feelings in words. For example, you might say, "I can see that you are angry and disappointed that your behavior is unacceptable."

4. Think of ways that you as a parent can provide outlets for the general gifted child problem of exceptional and widespread curiosity, because this is a long-range challenge.

5. Recognize that your child's "cleverness" or "smartness" about tangential issues can undermine your ability to set limits.

6. Start thinking of ways to avoid power struggles with your gifted child by making sure that the discipline you establish has a real purpose. Power struggles with young children are usually over arbitrary rules that have very little meaning to the child.

MARY AND THE MAGIC MARKERS: UNDERSTANDING AND TALKING TO A YOUNG CHILD WHO IS OVERCONCENTRATING OR OVERFOCUSED

Mary is an energetic five-year-old who loves to draw. She has a collection of colored pencils, crayons, watercolors, and every type of marker imaginable. When her grandparents recently returned from a vacation, they gave her a new type of "magic marker." Mary is fascinated by the new types of designs she can now make.

The day after acquiring the magic markers, Mary goes on vacation to the beach with her parents. She brings her magic markers. Mary can't stop drawing. She does not want to go to the beach or the pool. Mary prefers to stay in the hotel room and make new designs. Mom and dad are concerned that Mary is missing out on her vacation. They decide that Mary needs to go outside and swim and play in the sand. Mom says to Mary, "I can see that you are fascinated by your new magic markers." This statement affirms Mary's intense feelings about drawing and expressing herself. Then her mother sets a limit. She says, "It is time to put these markers away and go outside and play in the sunshine."

Mary is enraged that she has to put her markers away. Mary screams at her mother, "I am not going outside. I want to play with my markers. I don't care what you say." Both mom and dad are horrified at Mary's reaction to their well-thought-out, seemingly reasonable limit.

These thoughts and feelings go through her parents' minds:

1. Mom feels ashamed. She wonders, "Did we do something wrong as parents? Our daughter is way too headstrong and defiant." Dad points out, "Blaming ourselves for Mary's behavior will not help us settle this problem."

2. Dad is furious, and he suggests that it might help to throw the entire collection of markers in the trash. "We'll just take everything away from her. We'll teach her a lesson." Mom reminds her husband that Mary's drawing is a very important creative and intellectual outlet. Indeed, drawing is a way that children learn that they have the right to make their own decisions. Mom

also points out that punishment is a short-term solution to the problem at hand.

3. Mary's parents reject the option of shaming their daughter for being overly intense about drawing. They know that Mary is very sensitive and self-conscious, and that any type of personal insult will just further her insecurities.

Decision Point and Intervention

Both parents agree to be positive about Mary's ability to concentrate on a task. After they calm down, Mom and Dad together make a plan to set some realistic and healthy limits on Mary's creative behavior, which at times seems obsessive. They begin discussing their ideas about limits and boundaries with their daughter. They acknowledge Mary's love of drawing and creating designs, and tell her that they are very proud of her. "You are a wonderful artist," her mom says. Dad says, "I am proud of you for working so hard on your pictures." This statement positively acknowledges Mary's persistence.

Next, they set a limit on what might be described as Mary's perfectionist and obsessive behavior. Mom says, "Mary, there is a time and place for every activity. While we are on vacation is not a good or the right time to stay in the hotel and draw."

Dad says, "Mary, we are limiting your drawing time to late afternoon and after dinner. Otherwise we, as a family, will be outside at the beach."

Both parents hope they are prepared for their daughter's reaction. Mary is very upset. She starts to cry and sob. "You don't love me. You don't understand me. Why do I have to go outside?"

Dad and Mom help Mary. "We love you and understand that drawing is important. Still, we know what is best for you." (This is said in a calm and nonthreatening tone.)

At first, Mary is unhappy that she has to go outside during the day. She has clearly gotten the message that she is not the boss. However, Mary quickly makes friends at the pool and forgets her unhappiness. Mom and Dad remember because it will help them be firm when another situation arises.

"Good Enough" Communication

1. Listen to your child. Identify and acknowledge your child's feelings. Tell your child in an empathic voice that you understand how he or she is feeling.

2. Set appropriate child limits that take into consideration your child's developmental stage. For example, drawing is very important to children who are just starting kindergarten because it allows for self-expression and gives children a chance to make their own decisions.

3. Respond to your child's disappointment about having limits. Show empathy for her point of view. Don't just say, "No, this has got to stop because I say so."

4. Pay close attention to how you are feeling about the issues. Are you overidentified with your child's pain and disappointment? Were your parents too strict with you? What is motivating your response to your child?

5. Realize that a big difficulty of parenting a gifted child is dealing with his or her emotional intensity. The drama over whatever—food, markers, clothes, toys—is more easily diffused in a positive way when you don't give in and don't overreact.

CALVIN AND THE COMPUTER: SETTING LIMITS ABOUT PASSIONATE INTERESTS FOR A NINE-YEAR-OLD

Cal is a whiz kid on the computer. He is able to program and do very complicated graphics. His teachers at school encourage his parents to buy him a computer that is the most up-to-date model. There are advantages and disadvantages to the new purchase. Cal is able to do more programming and graphics, but he starts to fall behind in other academic areas. He spends most of his time glued to the monitor. He ignores his friends, refuses to do his homework, and stops doing household chores.

These feelings, thoughts, and possible actions run through his parents' minds:

1. "We are enraged. Let's lock up the new computer in the family
   safe."

2. "This is just too frustrating. Let's send Cal off to boarding
   school."

3. They feel hopeless about ever finding a solution to the issue of
   computer overuse. "We must have failed as parents, because
   our child is just too intense."

4. Dad thinks about shaming Cal and saying, "You should be happy
   that you got this computer. It cost me a lot of hard-earned
   money!" Mom reminds him that humiliation is the silent killer
   of self-esteem.

5. They realize that they need a new strategy. Cal is at a higher
   developmental stage. He needs to be a part of the decision-
   making process. What would other parents do in a similar
   situation?

Decision Point and Intervention

Cal's parents decide to talk to Cal about what is positive about his
attachment to the computer. They are aware that Cal is old enough
to have some input about how much time he needs to use his computer. Then they plan to develop a computer time-management
plan with their son. What does Cal think will be the optimal time
spent on the computer, as compared to how he will manage other
responsibilities with school, friends, and chores?

Cal's parents acknowledge his passionate interest. "You are re-
markably smart on the computer. You are a genius," Dad says, with
pride in his voice. "I'm delighted that you are enjoying our new
computer," his mother says, with less enthusiasm then her husband. Cal is happy that his parents understand his interest, and he
says quietly, "Thanks for getting the new computer."

Quickly his father says, "Can we find a way to work out the

problem of too much time on the computer? How much time do you think is enough time?" Cal is shocked by his father's question, because he is hoping for no restrictions. He is silent for a while and then gets a terribly sour look on his face. Cal says that he understands his parents' point of view. Still, he suggests an outrageous amount of time on the computer. After a long discussion of school, home, and family responsibilities, rules are made for computer use. These include specifics for what constitutes misuse, as well as consequences for not following the rules.

The entire family is happy with the plan for a week. Then a problem arises with overuse. Immediately, Dad follows through with the already decided upon consequences—no computer use for a week. Cal is very upset that he is being disciplined. He locks himself up in his room and refuses to come to dinner. He calls his grandparents for support and asks them to reason with his parents. But his starvation plan and grandparent conspiracy doesn't work out. His parents don't give in. He goes to bed hungry and slightly surprised that his parents didn't cave in: he is sure that they will relent in the morning.

Much to Cal's disappointment, the house rules stand and Cal loses his time on the computer for a week. His parents stand firm. An effective way to handle computer overuse has been established.

"Good Enough" Communication

1. Tell your child you understand how he or she feels about the computer. You might even say something about an interest you had as a child that was very compelling to you to bring your empathy even closer to home.

2. Calmly present your point of view with as much detail as your child can tolerate. Remember that presenting your point of view is very different from giving a lecture about your point of view.

3. Find out what your child believes are fair limits and take these into consideration.

4. Negotiate a compromise, as your child is old enough to have a voice in the decision.

5. Set limits that can be followed by the whole family.

6. Be prepared to enforce the rules if your child does not follow them.

RACHEL AND THE BLACK T-SHIRTS: TALKING TO A TEENAGE DAUGHTER ABOUT HER EMOTIONAL INTENSITY

Rachel is an outgoing and serious eighth grader. Her parents believe that she is developing a unique sense of herself. But she is also struggling, as all teenagers do, to fit in and be accepted by the other kids at school. An informal dress code of tattered tight jeans and black tee shirts is established by the eighth grade "in crowd." Rachel wants to look and feel like she belongs. She literally spends hours on the phone with friends talking about shopping for the right black shirt and jeans, as well as discussing the latest gossip.

Rachel's parents are sensitive to her teenage struggles to feel like she belongs and to develop her own identity. As long as Rachel can complete her homework and other responsibilities at home, her parents do not limit her time with her friends. Rachel understands her parents' expectations and continues to do very well at school. She is a straight-A student who never needs to be reminded to do her homework.

There is a problem in this seemingly happy family, however. Nearly every morning there is a crisis as Rachel gets ready for school. She is frantic as she looks for the right black shirt from her collection. Tears and anxiety about how she looks are common emotional states before school starts. Her parents are concerned and frustrated with their daughter's behavior as she continues her quest for the elusive, yet right "school uniform." Her father and brother stay out of her way. Her mother tries to stay positive and talks about how beautiful Rachel always looks no matter what she is wearing. Mother's attitude further infuriates Rachel. It seems as if there is no way to avoid a scene.

These thoughts and feelings run through her parents' minds:

1. Dad says angrily, "Let's send her to a private school where they are required to wear uniforms. The unofficial uniform of the 'in crowd' is causing way too much insanity in my house."

2. Mom feels sorry for Rachel. She thinks she knows how it feels to go through this type of peer pressure. Mom also worries that her daughter may be developing an obsession with her appearance. Mom worries that her own insecurities have been absorbed by her daughter. She is concerned that she is overidentified with her daughter's pain and that she is making a bad situation worse.

3. Both parents agree that they cannot take the daily morning hysteria.

Decision Point and Intervention

Mom and Dad decide that they need to first understand and then talk to their daughter about the importance of her informal dress code. Mom says in her calmest and most composed voice, "Rachel, I notice that you and your friends are collecting black shirts and ripped jeans. I think together you and your friends must have 30 black tee shirts that you share. I can't tell the differences between these black shirts. But I know how you think you look when you go to school is very important to you. Can you explain why you are so concerned about your appearance to your dad and to me?"

Rachel responds curtly and quickly, "You're right, mom, the way I look is the most important thing that happens in the morning." And in the same breath she adds, "Becky needs you to shorten and tighten her old jeans. Can you do it? Her mom doesn't know how to sew." Rachel says nothing about her morning scene, or why.

Dad is amused and proud of his daughter for speaking up. But he knows he needs to set some limits on the contagious morning anxiety that runs rampant in his home. "Your mother is very happy to help alter your jeans and your friend's jeans. But we are concerned with the amount of anxiety that is spread throughout the house when you are getting ready for school," he says. "How can we help you feel better about yourself?" Mom asks.

Rachel is enraged at her father and mother for bringing up the problem for discussion. "I can't believe you are expecting me to change because you say so! You know I don't respond to emotional commands!" she says in a highly agitated voice.

"Well, we *are* expecting some changes," her father says, "Get your clothes ready at night."

"Maybe this will help keep the morning calmer," her mother suggests.

Rachel gives her mother a seriously annoyed look and says, "I am not a five-year-old. That's what parents do with five-year-olds. I don't have time at night, anyway. I have way too much home-work. I like my morning routine."

Dad says sternly, "We don't like your stress spread around the house. You will lose your cell phone every evening that you act 'crazy' about your clothes." Mom adds, "It will be just fine with us if you get upset in your room alone and don't spread the anxiety around the house."

Rachel is furious. "Fine! Whatever you say!" She walks to her room and locks herself in. She calls Becky to tell her how mean her parents have been, adding that her mom has time to alter her jeans tonight.

The morning stress level is reduced because Rachel loses her cell phone when she tracks her anxiety throughout the house, so she quickly learns to contain herself.

"Good Enough" Communication

1. Tell your teenager that you are trying to understand how she feels and where she is coming from. Share a story from your teenage years that shows that you were a teenager once.

2. Calmly present your perspective. And be prepared to be ignored or even ridiculed.

3. Find out what your teenager thinks is fair. Listen carefully and attentively.

4. Set realistic limits that the entire family understands and can follow. Rules should take into consideration your teenager's safety and the well-being of the family.

5. Prepare yourself to listen to your son's or daughter's anger and disappointment. As important, set a limit to just how long you will listen.

6. Follow through on the stated consequences whenever necessary.

Strategies That Promote "Good Enough" Communication in the Family

Even though the ages of the children in the above stories are different and their issues with communication are developmentally unique, they demonstrate common parenting strategies that are effective.

1. The parents are attentive. Harry, Mary, Cal, and Rachel all know that their parents understand and accept how they are feeling.

2. Parental understanding and acceptance motivates the development of an open dialogue that includes talking about positive and negative experiences in the family.

3. All of these children are given fair or appropriate limits that reflect their particular stage of development and their needs for a healthy and safe life.

4. The parents are willing to listen to what their child feels is reasonable, even if they can't or won't go along with everything that their child may think is fair.

5. Limits are reasonable and easy to follow.

Discussion or talk between parent and child about acceptable and unacceptable behavior is the cornerstone of all good-enough parent–child bonds.

Be Honest

Communication is based on trust, and trust is based on honesty. Gifted children are very perceptive and sensitive to their parents' actions and reactions. They will have a good sense of any positive or negative situations or events very quickly. Whether you are excited, tired, anxious, or unhappy, they will sense your mood and look for clues around them to understand why. If you try to hide something from your child or exaggerate and embellish your opinion of the circumstances or a particular accomplishment, your child will know that something is not right. Dishonesty breeds mistrust and undermines positive communication between parent and child.

I am not suggesting that you have to tell your children all of the details of difficult situations or all of the possibilities of a wonderful situation. Child-appropriate explanations are extremely important. There is a wide range of options or approaches to choose from when you tell your child about a new situation or a new issue. Make sure your child can understand what new information you are explaining. *But don't avoid the truth* or make up a story because you feel that honest talk is too painful or embarrassing to share.

Avoid Threats

Threats are an insidious form of dishonesty that parents have used throughout the ages. Threats are usually unsuccessful because parents are not telling the truth. Let's look at some examples where threats accomplish nothing or are actually counterproductive.

1. Your children are fighting with each other in the car and you can't stand it. You scream at your children, "Stop it now or

I will turn around and go home." This works for a short time and then it starts all over again, because your kids know it is just a threat and you probably won't turn around and go home.

2. A mother threatens her five-year-old daughter into cleaning up her bedroom before school. She tells her to make her bed otherwise something "bad" might happen while she is at school. The clever child decides that she will never her make her bed because something "bad" could happen anyway and she will have wasted her play time making her bed. Her mother's threat does not promote a well-made bed or a neat bedroom—or honest communication and trust.

Avoid White Lies

Although parents easily can justify making up white lies, they create problems that undermine the parent–child relationship. This is another common approach to communicating with your child that does not work. Here are some possible scenarios:

1. The hurried and overwhelmed parent tells a child, "I'll be back in 10 minutes," and returns two hours later. The child then develops enormous separation anxiety when the parent leaves, even if it is supposedly for just for a very short time.

2. Mom and dad are having serious marital problems. They are angry or fighting with each other most of the time they are together. Their children are aware of the tension in the house. They ask each parent separately what is wrong. Dad says, "I'm just tired." Mom says, "I just need more time for myself." Their children see through these half truths. But, they reach for the wrong conclusions. They believe that their parents are unhappy with them. Their self-esteem suffers while their unacceptable behavior at school increases.

Be Attentive to Your Children

It seems so simple to just ask you to listen to and focus on what your child is saying as a way to improve positive communication. Unfortunately, most parents have a lot of difficulty just listening to their children. Their minds may be on other matters. They may be emotionally drained from the stress of the day. They can be preoccupied with financial worries. Whatever the obstacle to listening to your child, it will create a disconnect. The build-up of countless minor disconnects will lead to anger, arguments, and communication failures.

Let's look at some everyday examples of how routinely parents don't listen:

❑ Your children are fighting over a television show. The older one runs into the kitchen screaming, "I hate my brother!"

Undermining Reaction

Your immediate response is, "You don't really hate your brother. We have taught you to love one another." This response shows that you cannot accept your child's feelings of anger. It makes your child's anger go underground and directs it toward self-blame or into acting out bad behavior. You are telling your child that anger is shameful and unacceptable. You are breaking down the possibility for positive communication in the family.

"Good Enough" Reaction

"I can see that you are feeling really angry with your brother. What is going on between you? I am going to talk to both of you when I finish preparing dinner."

❑ You take your four-year-old to the zoo and he gets frightened by the bears. He starts crying and wants to get away from the bear cage.

Undermining Reaction

"You really are a super-sensitive child! We can't take you anywhere." This reaction totally ignores your child's feelings. It makes the child feel like he is not entitled to his feelings. You are telling your child that feelings are shameful. You are also lowering your child's self-esteem.

"Good-Enough" Reaction

"I can see that the bears really scared you. I am glad that you took your feelings seriously and walked away from the cages. Next time we come to the zoo, we will not go to look at the bears unless you want to." This reaction validates your child's feelings. It teaches your child to trust his feelings and to use them as a signal that something is scary and should be avoided.

❑ You and your husband love the Discovery Channel. You tell your eight-year-old daughter to watch a program about butterflies. Your daughter is bored and tells you so.

Undermining Reaction

"You should like the Discovery Channel. That program on butterflies was just so beautiful. There is no reason for you to complain." You are simply telling your child that her feelings are not important. This is the wrong message to give a child when you want to develop trust.

"Good-Enough" Reaction

"I am glad you shared your feelings with me. Why don't we watch a TV program or a movie that you like?" This reaction tells your child that you are interested in her feelings. It will allow you to talk about her interests, which will in turn develop her sense of herself.

Talk in a Language Your Child Can Understand

Of course, this means that you should try not to lecture or talk down to your child. (I realize this is a prescription that may, at times, be hard to follow.) There is just no point in talking over your child's head. Still, parents can have a hard time being attentive and speaking in a way that their children can understand or relate to in a nonthreatening way.

With the gifted child this challenge is even harder because sometimes smart kids can understand and respond to adult language. At other times when they are feeling more vulnerable, they will shut down to a more immature state of mind. When your children are acting their stated age, they need to be spoken to in a more compassionate and understanding way. When your children are in an expansive state of mind, it is fine to talk to them as an adult. You will need to learn how to switch communication gears quickly from adult to child if you are going to talk in a language they can understand.

Set Limits Without Anger

Gifted children definitely try your will to discipline them because they can be so opinionated and relentless. When you are composing the household rules, you should be firm. If you are angry, try to keep it to yourself, because you will be more effective. Think about it. Why are you so angry about setting a limit? Are your expectations too high? Limits should be based on what a particular situation calls for, not an arbitrary standard. For example, a clean room for a child is very different that a clean child's room pictured in a magazine.

Parents of gifted children often have more problems with discipline because their children are very good at talking, but their listening skills and judgment are not always at an optimal place.

Smart children like to make up their own rules, and they don't and won't understand that they are not as smart as their parents. They can be infuriating. It may be very hard to do, but try not to take your child personally.

Be Available

Typical children require a lot of attention from their parents! Gifted children require even more attention because of their curiosity and energy level. It is one thing to say you are available and another to actually be available. *If you are serious,* you will turn off your cell phone when you are spending time with your child.

Today's parents give their children mixed messages about their availability because of their own frantic life agendas. Mixed messages make children angry and teach them not to trust you. Next time you tell your child you want to spend quality time together, be sure you don't lose your focus, which is on your child. Likewise, when you can't be with your child, you need to be clear that you are not available and forget your guilt that you are not 100 percent available. See Chapter 2 about good-enough parenting.

Avoid Power Struggles

When discipline is appropriate and practical you will have fewer problems with power struggles. Fighting with a gifted child can be a serious emotional trial for the entire family. Still, acknowledging to your child and to yourself that power struggles are common is a good starting point. Remember that the rules you make up should benefit the entire family.

Don't casually undermine your spouse or other people in authority. You need to teach your children to respect other people. The best way to do this is to treat your spouse, grandparents, teachers, and other the professionals in your family life with the respect they deserve. When children see their parents being devaluing, critical, or indifferent to others in authority, they learn that it is acceptable to be disrespectful. Antagonism against authority is one lesson you don't want your smart children to learn from you, because it will make your child even more difficult to talk to and it will undermine appropriate socialization skills. Smart kids who understand the importance of respect are sure to be successful in developing their own potential.

Value Cooperative Family Time

Definitely find time to have dinner together, go to the movies, museums, and vacations. A family that has fun together and works on projects or chores together is able to function as a unit and provide the necessary structure for their child to grow socially. A working communication system is a necessary outcome of cooperative family time. Cooperative family time teaches your child how to interact with others, which is a valuable life skill.

Respect Your Child's Struggles

Everybody struggles. It is a part of life. Gifted children come to understand the meaning of their struggles the hard way. They are quick, and learning comes easily to them. They don't like struggling and they try to avoid it. You have to allow your child to learn how to struggle.

Boredom is a gifted child's biggest and most common struggle. Ninety-eight percent of the parents I talk with ask what they can do about their child's boredom. I always respond the same way. Gifted children get bored easily and they definitely and absolutely must learn to deal with not always being challenged— in other words, with being bored. They need to learn how to do routine tasks.

Encourage Independence

You can encourage independence by not overidentifying with your child. Ask yourself, "Is my child afraid to be home alone, or am I afraid to leave my child alone? Is my child afraid to be left with his grandparents for the weekend, or is leaving my child uncomfortable for me?"

Using the same line of reasoning, don't overreact to your child's anxiety about trying new experiences. Encourage your gifted child to try new things, but do not push. Role modeling reasonable risk-taking behaviors is an excellent way to teach your child to be independent.

Where and when it is possible, give your child choices. Allowing for options encourages independence. Common ways children are given choices are in the selection of books, play dates, enrichment classes, short family outings, and special projects.

Be Positive

Being a positive parent is crucial to opening up family dialogue. Parents who are negative put a damper on their child's ability to talk about or try new experiences or to explore their creativity. Parents who are critical teach by their own example nonacceptance of others and fearfulness. Gifted children are intense and sensitive to negative cues from their parents. When children learn to be shy and fearful or antagonistic, their capacity to talk to their parents and teachers is seriously diminished.

Show Your Child That You Are Proud

Praise your son or daughter when they accomplish a task or develop their talent, or show kindness and sensitivity to others. Encouragement and applause are crucial ways to improve your child's self-esteem. Emotionally supportive parents can help their children open up about their feelings. A child who receives enough praise is less likely to be fearful and more able to be creative.

Roadblocks to Open Communication with Gifted Children

From my experiences working with very smart parents with very bright children, I have observed the following roadblocks that need to be removed if communication is going to move forward.

Roadblock 1: Parents Long for "Easy" Communication

Parents of gifted children long for communication with their son or daughter to be easier. But more often than not, it is difficult to communicate with your smart child, which can seem to be in sharp contrast to your child's amazing insight and knowledge about many subjects.

Probably the most common and frustrating problem that parents and gifted children have is dealing with boredom. All too often gifted children complain or daydream, and they cannot explain why. Parents are left to guess what is wrong. Teachers ask, "Does your child have attention deficit disorder?"

A prime example of a communication roadblock is when you ask your child a general question like, "What's happening?" "What are you doing now?" The child or teenager, or even the young adult, replies, "Stuff." You may be put off by this evasive response. After dealing with countless roadblocks, the smart parent realizes the advantages or disadvantages of simply dropping the question and not probing any further. I assure you there are no right or objective ways to deal with the evasive answers. Practicality reigns here. If you have time, or it is crucial to your child's health and safety, try to understand what your child is trying to hide. If not, accept the "stuff" answer and go on.

Roadblock 2: Emotional Intensity of the Gifted Child Makes Communication Difficult

Parents of very smart children think because they have little geniuses that talking about what's bothering them should be easier. I have heard so many parents say to me, "I know my son is smart; it should be easy for him to tell me why he is so upset." I say to the parent, "You are wrong when you think it should be easier. Your child's emotional intensity makes it more difficult for him or her to communicate with you."

As an example, your child loses his homework somewhere between school and home and comes into the house very upset. You ask, "What's wrong?" It is hard to get an answer on this one. Your child may be angry at himself, his friends, the teacher, or you for asking the question. Maybe your child is not sure why he is so upset. It is not easy to get to the bottom of the problem because your child's perfectionism and sensitivity to making mistakes will intensify and, in turn, his capacity to explain himself will diminish or even shut down.

Roadblock 3: Parents Can Get Confused About Where to Set the Limit

Gifted children are complicated and intense. Their reactions to people, places, and interactions are vivid and complex. They can and very often will look at and talk about all aspects of a situation, which is quite distracting when you are trying to set a limit. You need to focus on safety and practicality when your child overwhelms you with details and arguments that are tangential to the real issue. For example, "I told you we are not going to the concert in town. It is too late for a school night." Your six-year-old replies, "My piano teacher said that going to concerts was so important for my education as a pianist. All the kids in class are going. I want to see the performance. I know it will help me play the piano better."

Your answer is still "No way."

Roadblock 4: Gifted Parents Have the Same Problems as Their Children

Parents of very bright children are usually very talented and effective people themselves. They tend to have the same problems as their children with perfectionism, sensitivity, seeing all aspects of the issue, and not being able to prioritize what is most important. You will be more effective if you can make a plan and focus on what issue is to be discussed with your child. Parents who get scattered and resonate with every idea their child brings up will lose their authority and be totally exhausted and ineffective. In other words, give up your perfectionistic tendencies.

Your Smart Kids Have a Hard Time with You, Too

You may think that you are the most reasonable and loving parent. And maybe you are. So you don't see why your gifted child should have any trouble communicating with and understanding you. But your smart kid will still have a hard time with you, for the following reasons.

They Think They Are Smarter Than You

I know this from countless experiences talking to gifted children and raising two as well. And in my experience there is no way to change their deep-seated belief that they are right and you—their parents—are wrong until they face real-life issues as adults.

My adult son, Richard, shared his thoughts on the subject of being a know-it-all and how he came to understand that he was not smarter than me.

> "I think this is why I thought that I was smarter than you and dad. It was the intersection of your perfectionism as parents with my perfectionism. Within the parent–child bond, the child

lacks in one area and the parent lacks in another way. For example, I was very good at taking care of myself and my sister in the late afternoon if you were at school and dad was at the office. I excelled in many other areas as well, and you allowed these parts of me to grow and develop. Your pride in my accomplishments helped your sense of self as a parent and in practical ways as well. I knew that you believed in me and that gave me great courage to try new things.

"I could not understand or learn that my judgment was lacking an adult dimension. At times I was resentful because I thought I was raising my parents. You were at times resentful that I was so open about being a know-it-all kid. The hardships that you endured and the hardships that I endured being a know-it-all were significant. When we let go of our anger at each other there was a resolution. This resolution usually begins in young adulthood when the gifted child realizes that he does want to be a kid instead of an undergrown adult. By wanting to just be a child there is a realization that your parents have their own problems and they are not perfect."

Gifted children enjoy being highly articulate and communicative when it works for them—when they want to talk. Remember, you are not in control of when your child feels like talking to you. If your child is reluctant to answer, it is better not to pressure them into talking. It is totally unproductive to manipulate them into talking to you by saying, "I wish you would talk like you usually do."

They Enjoy Arguing

Arguing is an intellectual challenge for gifted children; it is something they really enjoy. They don't and really can't understand that they are driving you crazy. However, they don't need to *understand* how you feel about dealing with their insistent behavior. They need to learn to be quiet if you ask them to stop arguing.

They Don't Understand Adult Limits, but They Think They Do

Smart kids are know-it-alls, which means they think they understand everything, although they really don't. Your gifted children need to follow the rules or expectations you establish, even if they think they know better than you. They don't have all the answers. Judgment lags behind reasoning, which is why gifted children have a hard time respecting adults.

Their Emotional Intensity Interferes with Their Capacity to Cope

Smart kids' emotional intensity can be overwhelming and will interfere with the logical and intellectual aspects of their personality. Refer back to Chapter 4 for examples of how emotional intensity diminishes their ability to cope with problems.

Hard Issues to Talk About with Your Gifted Child

Obviously, some issues are really hard to talk with *any* child about. The parents of gifted children I work with share some of these issues:

"It is hard to talk about mortality for obvious reasons. I don't want my son thinking about my death or his own, just like I don't like thinking about it. He did tell me he wanted the two of us to die on the same day so he wouldn't have no mommy."   Angela

"The hardest issue to discuss with my daughter is why she works so slowly in class (though she does this at home, too). I think much of it comes from her perfectionism. She often has impossibly high standards for herself and others. She will get angry and frustrated if I don't immediately understand the idea she is trying to convey or what she wants me to do."   Tanya

"The hardest thing to talk about with my twin daughters is the divorce. I don't want them to think it is their fault. It had nothing to do with them. I don't want them to blame themselves. I can see the pain of divorce in their eyes. I am saddened that we couldn't stay together and be a family. Not having a daddy in the home must be hard for them."   Isabella

"My son and I have different hard issues. Homework is very hard for Jake to talk about. For me, it's our impending divorce."   Mary

"The hardest topic I have to talk to my five-year-old daughter about is sex. She was extremely curious. I was concerned about sharing too much detail with her. I got some children's books on sexuality and talked with my parenting group about what they would say. When she asked me to explain sex to her I kept it simple. I did not rely on the stork story."   Julia

"The hardest thing to talk to my son about is his perfectionism. I tell him countless times and ways that he does not need to be perfect. He cannot listen to me. He just wants things to go perfectly, the way he wants, or not at all. This is true with food, clothes, piano, activities, and homework. There seems to be no solution. Other topics are effortless."   George

"It is easy to talk to him about most issues. We have never had problems with discipline because he wanted to get our approval. Emotional issues are the most challenging. He is very sensitive. In preschool, one of his friend's mom died. He knew his friend was not going to have a mommy and he knew what that meant. I was concerned about explaining death to him the right way. He understands that death is a permanent situation. Adults have similar issues understanding death."   Cindy

Communicating with Your Gifted Child

Learning to talk to and communicate with children in a way that develops and enhances their self-esteem and their sense of themselves is crucial and challenging. Accepting your child's feelings and empathizing with their success as well as their struggles is the basis of an open-ended dialogue. Establishing fair discipline that can be followed keeps the channels of communication between you and your child open. When communication inevitably breaks down, look for the causes of misunderstanding and renegotiate a plan to keep your children talking to you about what is meaningful to them.

Instant Tips for Talking to Your Smart Kid

1. Sometimes it is a lot of fun and other times it is much harder than you want it to be. And that is just how it is.

2. Keep focused on the real issue. If you get distracted by side issues, your life will be much harder.

3. Don't always believe everything you are told by your smart kids. Smart kids are very convincing, but sometimes they are wrong. For example, your child says she needs to dissect a frog, then a fetal pig, then a person. She really doesn't need to do this.

CHAPTER SIX

Developing Your Child's
Unique Potential

Giftedness has to be discovered and developed. Educational researchers teach us that "talent" does not flourish on its own. As a parent, you must learn to nurture what is unique in your gifted child. Giftedness is a condition that can be developed in some children only if an appropriate interaction takes place between the child, his or her environment, and a particular area of human endeavor.

Joseph Renzulli, a well-known and respected educator of gifted children, states:

"It should be kept in mind that when I describe . . . a certain trait as being a component of giftedness (for example, creativity), I am in no way assuming that one is 'born with' this trait, even if one happens to possess a high IQ. Almost all human abilities can be developed, and therefore my intent is to call attention to the potentially gifted (that is to say, those who could 'make it' under the right conditions) as well as to those who have been studied because they gained some type of recognition. Implicit in this concept of the potentially gifted, then, is the idea that giftedness emerges or 'comes out' at different times and under different circumstances."

You need to try to understand and hopefully believe in this very important statement about the nature of the gifted child's potential. Giftedness is not a flower that magically blooms without water. The gifted child must be nurtured to reach his or her potential.

Potential Is Not Enough: Ensure Your Child a Richness of Experience

Developing your child's unique potential is one of the most important issues you face as the parent of a gifted child. This uncharted area is your own personal challenge. You and your spouse or significant other are really on your own. There are no road maps to follow, although you can glean knowledge from other parents, educators, and even gifted adults. The most valuable source of information will be your child's interests and inclinations.

While still attending to the day-to-day school and home issues, you need to encourage your child to find his or her passions. Early interests or passions can be the underpinnings of your child's unique potential and eventual genius. True passion often begins with collecting items such as dolls, stamps, toys, rocks, cars, or having a special interest in dance, science, music, or art. Allowing and encouraging your child's curiosities is critical to later intellectual development, self-esteem, and creativity.

The outside enrichment activities, the books you choose to read or give to your child, travel adventures, and quality family experiences that you expose your child to are the foundation of future adult identity. Parents often ask me, "How will I know what to do to help my child find his true interests to find himself? How much time should I spend doing art versus science versus foreign language?" I always tell parents that the answer is in you and in your child—and between you and your child.

Raising a gifted child is like planting and caring for a special garden. Beautiful and complicated gardens need gardeners who make careful decisions and plans about what to plant, given the soil quality, sunshine available, and the rainfall patterns. A garden has to be reevaluated after each growing season, after the gardener gets a sense of what is doing well and what is not thriving. Good-enough gardeners know the importance of being sensitive to what is doing well in their garden and what is not doing well and why. This is how it should be with good-enough parents of gifted children.

In my experience, if you are tuned into your child's individual needs and are able to objectively assess and subjectively try to understand your child's progress at a task, you will be successful at raising your gifted child. Responsive parents who have learned how to advocate for their children and who have a flexible plan for how they are going to nourish them so that they can flourish get the best long term results.

In contrast, parents who use their children as status symbols of their own genius or who deny or ignore their children's particular giftedness are the least successful. I am including in this unsuccessful category the parents who are overidentified with their children, and give them what they *think* their children need instead of doing the work of identifying what their children actually need. Parents who don't tune into their children's gifts generally have serious problems with them in adolescence. As adults, children who have underdeveloped talents or who have not learned to deal with their uniqueness are very often alienated or depressed and live troubled lives.

Understanding How to Motivate Your Child

You're on the right road to raising your gifted child to feel good about who he or she is if you make decisions about the child's development based on your observations. Psychologically minded parents—those who consider what is motivating or not motivating their children—seem to develop the most interesting, unique, and effective educational plans. Let's look at how some of these psychologically minded parents provide the creative, motivational, and intellectual structure for their child's unique development.

The Nilsson Family

Ben Nilsson, who was introduced in Chapter 2, is a child who definitely needs the right kind of stimulation in school. He is very sensitive to his teachers' expectations or lack thereof. His mother sums up her son's problems at school by saying, "Either the teachers see him as a beautiful, brilliant, gifted child, or they don't know what to do with him. Ben can be highly distracted, marching to his own drummer, not paying attention, and challenging the teacher's authority."

Ben's mom and dad are concerned parents who understand their son's reactivity to the right school environment. When his family moves to California, Ben is placed in a top-of-the-line politically correct public school. Ben is bored beyond belief at this supposedly fabulous school. He can't relate to his teachers and starts to withdraw his attention from school. His parents speak with the principal and Ben's teachers at the public school and decide that Ben needs a smaller classroom, more individual attention, and a more complicated and enriched curriculum.

Fortunately, Ben is accepted at a small private school in their neighborhood. He has a great deal of anticipatory anxiety about making new friends, but not about the academics. His mother says, "My kid can use half of his brains and still get Bs." His parents understand his anxiety and reassure him that he will still be able to see his old friends from the neighborhood public school. They monitor Ben's adjustment to the new school, which seems to go smoothly. Enrichment activities after school are selected in Ben's area of interests, which include art, sports, and music. Ben attends gifted children's summer camps and travels with his family.

Mrs. Nilsson shares the following thoughts: "We are trying to avoid the 'drill and kill' that is found in today's schools. Ben is not an auditory learner. The pace at his school is too slow. It is really difficult to find a school that meets his intellectual needs. We want a school that will offer socialization opportunities. A school where the teachers are emotionally nurturing. We are trying to let him pursue his deep intellectual interests outside of the school environment with tutors and other types of mentors."

The O'Hara Family

Isabella O'Hara, like the other parents who are described in this book, is highly gifted and motivated. She knows how bright her twin children are and what they like to do academically and creatively. When they are three years old, Carrie and Amy attend the church preschool in their neighborhood. They are bored at preschool and tell their mother how they feel about school during their morning "questions and comments time."

Isabella takes her children seriously. She talks with the teachers and the director of the preschool. Defensively, school educators tell Isabella that all children, including her twins, need to focus on more social and emotional issues and less on parental academic pressure. In contrast, Isabella says to the director, "My children are sick of just looking at rocks. They need to be stimulated." The director tells Isabella that academic issues are not important and insinuates that she is a pushy mother. These hostile comments from the director do not detour this smart mom, who starts looking at other preschool options in her community that will more actively engage her twins.

Meanwhile, Mrs. O'Hara finds outside enrichment activities for her girls to explore, awaken, and extend their interests. Carrie and Amy go to a reading group for preschoolers, dance classes, tennis, and Spanish lessons. During the summer they attend summer camps that focus on art and mathematics, which reflects each child's interests. These twins travel with their family and have frequent play dates with other children, including other twins. Isabella is looking for a good piano teacher for her girls.

Mrs. O'Hara skips her four-year-old twins a grade to a private kindergarten. After researching all of the gifted private and public schools in her community, she wants to continue accelerating her children into a public school first grade. Carrie and Amy are socially astute, developing their own individuality, and are at the head of their class in academics.

The Owen Family

Michelle and David Owen, who were introduced in Chapter 3, are very attentive and psychologically minded parents. Their son Noah begins kindergarten at the neighborhood public school. An individualized education plan (IEP) is completed by the school district to assess Noah's special needs. As Noah has a previous diagnosis of autistic spectrum disorder, a part-time shadow teacher is provided for two months as Noah makes the transition to this new school. Noah does beautifully in kindergarten and at the after-school enrichment. He is able to make friends on his own and excels in academics. After three months, the specialists and the teachers at this public school do not see any need for extra help in the classroom. Rather, they suggest to Michelle that Noah is very bright and they want to place him in the gifted component, which starts in first grade.

Michelle is delighted that Noah is doing so well socially on his own. Still, she cannot give up her quest for acceptance at the perfect private school. When Noah tells his mother that he wants to stay at the public school until fifth grade, Michelle relents and Noah stays in the public school of his choice. Michelle continues with Noah's enrichment activities, which include art, music, and sports. Noah is enrolled in a summer camp for gifted children, and he really enjoys this experience. Play dates with children from school and camp are continuous throughout the year. The family travels together to visit relatives and friends, to attend museums, and sometimes to just relax.

The Cramer Family

Jacob Cramer, who was introduced in Chapter 2, attends a project-centered private elementary school that is focused on each child's individual development. The parents are required to read a best-selling book, *A Mind at a Time* by Mel Levine, on how to parent by seeing your child as an individual. As a first grader, Jacob is an avid reader and loves mathematics. The classroom teacher, after assessing Jacob's strengths, places him in second and third grade reading and math groups so that he is able to work at his level of achievement. Jacob stays with the first graders for all other subjects because his social maturity is not as advanced as his intellectual maturity.

Jacob has a host of different after-school enrichment activities because of the diversity of his interests. Dr. and Mrs. Cramer try to carefully select the "right" enrichment activities for their son. Jacob seems to really enjoy his piano lessons on a regular basis. Swimming and karate are also on his schedule. Family vacations always involve educational activities for Jacob.

Dr. Cramer explained to me that he and his wife have established four distinct pathways to developing Jacob's giftedness:

1. They read to their son and fill his life with books because they know the importance of the printed word to the gifted child. Books are used as an alternative to television.

2. Jacob is exposed to a broad array of cultural activities to develop his intellect, encourage his creativity, and find his unique interests.

3. Dr. and Mrs. Cramer support the school by volunteering in the classroom and working with all of the children.

4. They believe in nurturing Jacob's interests so they do not follow a prescriptive, overly orchestrated cookbook approach.

The Ray Family

Claire, who was discussed in Chapter 3, first went to private school for a short time, and then attended a neighborhood public school for most of the kindergarten year. Beverly, her mother, noticed that she was beginning to underachieve. Claire was misspelling words that she had already mastered and making silly mistakes to fit in with the other kids in her classroom.

Beverly decided to speak with the head of a local religious school in her community about Claire. The administrators at this Catholic school agreed to take Claire in May for the last month of kindergarten. If Claire was as capable as her parents claimed, she would be accelerated to second grade in fall.

Claire did very well at her new school. She made new friends and got back to work on her academics. Claire spent her summer afternoons with tutors so that she would be ready for second grade. And sure enough, she was ready. Claire, who has been accelerated by one whole grade, is still at the top of her second- grade class. She does extremely well with competition, as she enjoys being a high achiever. The teachers and administrators are careful not to push Claire. They attend carefully to her social and emotional development.

Mr. and Mrs. Ray are delighted that Claire is thriving in the structured and competitive environment of their community religious school. Mr. and Mrs. Ray are actively involved with the Parent Teacher Association. Claire continues with her active social schedule of play dates. All types of family activities remain a constant in Claire's life. Her outside enrichment is focused on her interests in dance and gymnastics.

The Rinaldi Family

Mr. and Mrs. Rinaldi are both attorneys specializing in litigation. They have two gifted children who have very different personalities and different talents. Linda, the older child, is extremely outgoing. She loves competition and performance. Languages are of special interest to her as well. Linda loves to be with her friends. She adapts easily to most environments that are compelling for her. Linda has a hard time with boredom.

From preschool through third grade, Linda attended an international school where two languages were taught in the classroom. She studied music and dance. The family moved when Linda was in fourth grade. Her parents placed her in a highly gifted private school, where she is surrounded by other highly talented children. Linda is doing very well in this accelerated environment. She continues her outside interests in music, dance, language, and drama.

Marie, the younger daughter who is more introspective and less outgoing than her sister, also attended a dual-language preschool. She has many friends at school, as well as imaginary friends, which is also common for some highly introspective gifted children. She attends the same highly gifted private school as her sister, where she is doing very well in her more quiet way. Marie enjoys playing with a few children at a time. She loves music and drawing.

Both children travel abroad with their family and are exposed to many different cultures and people. Their home life is unstructured and noncompetitive. However, both children are expected to complete their homework for the competitive school that they attend.

The Goodwin Family

Corin Barsley Goodwin, founder of Gifted Home Scholars Forum, writes:

"My family never planned to home school. After all, we thought, wasn't home schooling for left-wing freaks and right-wing religious zealots? As it turned out, we had an important lesson to learn, which would demolish the myths of who home schools, as we went through the process of creatively educating our highly gifted, twice-exceptional children.

"My daughter hit all the 'normal' developmental milestones very early, and was an avid and self-taught reader since the age of three years old. She attended a parent participation nursery school, and we could see that she was smarter than some of the other kids, but there were a number of other bright kids in the class, as well. We were proud of her intelligence, but did not yet equate it with anything other than an ability to master academic skills slightly ahead of the curve. When she was five years old, we dutifully began researching kindergartens in our area. We briefly considered private schools, but we crossed them off of our list, along with playing the lottery to pay for them. That left us, we thought, with just the public school option. We figured we had a choice between a neighborhood school or one of the alternative schools in the district.

"The public school classrooms did not seem to me to be environments where my daughter would be nurtured in a manner appropriate to her individual needs, but rather, places that would simply address the mean ability level and continue to crank out high test scores with the collateral damage of losing a handful of students on either end of the curve each year. I did not want my daughter to be one of those children, nor my son once he arrived at school age. I was left wondering what else to do.

"I knew a few families who had chosen home schooling, but until this point I had written off the idea as something just a little weird. It was certainly not what *my family* was going to do! Nonetheless, I felt pushed into exploring the possibilities, and after joining a local home school support group and attending their activities, as well as a statewide home school conference, my husband and I were convinced that home schooling was worth a try.

"We stuck with home schooling for the kindergarten year, doing nothing especially academic but allowing for child-led learning, and went back to the school district for a WIAT [Wechsler Individual Achievement Test] assessment at the end of the school year. The results were a significant spread between high and low scores, both of which were well into the gifted range. Long story short, the school psychologist who administered the test told us that the school could do nothing for my little girl and they recommended we continue home schooling. At last, we were in agreement!"

Different Reactions but Common Principles

Each of these families selected different schooling options for their child that range from a highly structured religious school to a very unstructured home schooling environment. Yet all of these families have important similarities:

1. They see their child as a gifted individual who needs special attention.
2. They look at the whole child and want to nurture social, emotional, academic, and physical aspects of his or her development.
3. They are involved with their child's school and enrichment activities on a regular basis.
4. They know how their child learns.
5. They recognize their child's strengths and limitations.
6. They consider traditional and nontraditional learning environments.

7. They believe in enrichment, acceleration, and camp experiences as crucial aspects of their child's education.

8. They value family life and family learning experiences.

9. They encourage their children to think creatively by exposing them to classes and experiences that will develop their interests as well as abstract and divergent thinking.

The wide range of decisions made by these parents shows us about the wide variety of talents and personalities that gifted children demonstrate and the lack of "rightness" of one particular approach to developing potential. The diversity of options and decisions shown here also indicates how parental values and beliefs about how to educate a child play a prominent role in education.

Obstacles to Your Child's Potential

Gifted children are hard to raise. I know that I am repeating myself here, but I want to belabor this point as it relates to your child's potential. The sensitivity of your gifted child is remarkable and amazing, and also makes your child more vulnerable to being hurt or disappointed by others. Hypersensitivity to being misunderstood or criticized by others is a prominent reason why stories of the lives of gifted adults can sometimes be tragic, horrifying—and it is the reason it is so important to develop tools that will help your child bloom into a successful adult

The prodigy who could not relate to other people; the genius who believed that he was a failure; the gifted child who is truly afraid to try to be genuinely good at something—I see these commonly told stories of lost souls in search of themselves as related to and reflective of the complicated issue of the relationship between achievement and emotional intensity. The way the emotional component of achievement is intertwined with the actualization of talent, genius, or great success can be difficult to under-stand—even for highly educated and enlightened individuals. Is there something truly elusive about the unfolding of genius? I think so!

We can try to delineate and understand how overachievement is related to underachievement and burnout. Overachievement is, in most instances, the polar opposite of underachievement. How-ever, overachievement can lead to burnout, which naturally leads to an inability to perform the talent the individual has developed—which, of course, eventually means underachievement.

Overachievement

My definition of *overachievement* is a very narrow focus on achieve-ment that is not based on a passionate, internalized interest. But overachievement has different real and emotional meanings to dif-ferent people. There are countless books and articles about achieve-ment. Clearly, some individuals value overachievement because it leads to all types of great success, wealth, or high status. The secret problem with overachievement is that it can be a way of covering up deep insecurities in a driven person.

Overachievement in children is usually a compensatory or overdetermined way of pleasing parents and teachers. Unfortu-nately, overachievement can later lead to burnout and under-achievement. In other words, the child is achieving to please others and to get the attention of others. There is not enough personal in-vestment in the overachievement for the child. The child becomes overly reliant on the praise of others, which is disastrous when the child encounters difficulties. The overachieving child will take any lack of success very seriously, and will not have the skills, com-mitment, or emotional wherewithal to try and try again. Let's look at some examples of how overachievement can lead to under-achievement and burnout.

JUSTIN THE GYMNAST

As a young child, Justin shows talent in gymnastics. His parents strongly encourage his talent as well as his academic achievement. As a teenager, Justin becomes a star on his high school gymnastics team. Justin loves the attention he receives from others for his all-star performances and he works very hard on his routine—he practices long hours before and after school. His effort pays off, and Justin receives an athletic scholarship to a fine college.

In college, Justin is no longer the best on his team. College sports are much more competitive. He feels very defeated when he is not winning the most applause from his audience and the highest scores in all events. Justin lowers his standards and focuses on being the best in only one event. Gradually, as his performances lose the praise they once received, Justin gives up his interest in gymnastics completely. After college, he announces that he is burnt out and quits gymnastics altogether. Justin uses his college education to work as an elementary school teacher.

JANE THE CLASS VALEDICTORIAN

Jane is the class valedictorian at her high school graduation. Her transcripts reveal that she has been excellent in all of her academic subjects and nonacademic pursuits. As a child, she was a prolific reader. She won all the school spelling bees. As a teenager, she becomes a star member of the debate team. Jane excels with little or no effort in almost everything she tries. She learns to love competing and being the best because of the attention she receives from parents, friends, and teachers.

Jane follows all of the advice she receives from parents, counselors, and teachers. Jane joins all the right clubs on campus. She participates in community service, while managing to attain a 4.0 grade point average including her honors courses. With attention to performing well, she attains a perfect score on the SAT. The fact that she is accepted at Harvard University, her first choice school, is not a shock to Jane and her family. What is clearly unexpected, however, is Jane's difficulty at Harvard.

Jane is unable to adjust to college life. She is no longer the smartest kid, which is troubling and confusing for her. Jane does not know how to fit in with the other students if she is not the best. Quickly, she becomes depressed and leaves college after two horrific months. After several years of psychotherapy in her home town, she returns to a community college to pursue her education. She gives up her quest for an Ivy League education and resolves to find herself.

Both Jane and Justin are overachievers who have difficulties following through, for two reasons. First, they only know how to be the best. Second, they are not truly passionate about their interests and talents. Unfortunately, they are dependent on the secondary attention they receive in the form of praise and pleasing their parents and teachers. They suffer from emptiness and depression when they don't get first place because they are overfocused on the external rewards of their performance or achievement. They truly lack an inner conviction.

Underachievement

We learn from the life struggles of gifted individuals that underachievement may be a necessary evil. Underachievement makes gifted people realize who they really are in relationship to others—some who are not as talented, quick, perfectionistic, and driven.

Underachievement may have different manifestations in different situations or contexts. It is usually a strong emotional reaction to an event or experience that a gifted person cannot think through. Here are some examples that illustrate early underachievement:

1. Jon, a five-year-old who can read at an eighth-grade level, is placed in a kindergarten with children who don't even know the alphabet. Jon does not know how to cope with the classroom situation, which is boring to him. He refuses to go to school because the other children are picking on him and calling him *bookworm*.

2. George, a seven-year-old, shows talent as a pianist. When George makes a mistake at his recital, he leaves the stage and refuses to go back and play. For several months he ignores his piano lessons.

3. Steve, a nine-year-old, is good in all of his academic subjects. Unfortunately, his handwriting is atrocious and he refuses to practice. He tells his parents that writing is too hard.

4. Lisa, a brilliant 15-year-old, can easily get all As in her honors classes. Her best friend takes ill and leaves school. Lisa shuts down because she is devastated by the absence of her friend. She does not hand in her homework and gets very poor grades.

5. Robert, a talented writer and film student, attends college classes that are disappointing and boring. He does not finish his first year of college at the school of his choice.

6. Beth, a perfectionistic senior, goes to an Ivy league college. She has difficulty with a psychology class, becomes fearful of failure, and gives up on the class and her interest in psychology.

Underachievement is a state of mind for a gifted individual that signals emotional distress with a particular learning task. Boredom, intense perfectionism, or an intense preoccupation with being the best, an inability to do simple tasks, and disappointment with a teacher or school or a job can all trigger the retreat into underachievement.

Burnout: When Achievement Issues Threaten to Shatter the Self

Early burnout is clearly an emotional problem that is related to overachievement or performance issues. The deeper the emotional issue, which usually involves overidentification with the parent, the more serious the overachievement/underachievement issue. To illustrate this point I will present two case histories of gifted individuals who were forced to give up their deeply passionate commitment to their art form because of unresolved emotional issues and a serious lack of socialization in childhood. These issues led to glaring career problems and an abrupt inability to achieve in their area of talent.

DEIDRE, THE BALLERINA

Deidre was performing with the Bolshoi Ballet, the Geoffrey Ballet, and American Ballet Theater as a teenager. Her strength, beauty, and grace were remarkable. It seemed like her career as a prima ballerina was inevitable.

Deidre started studying ballet at the age of three. By the time she was five years old, she took dance classes every day after school. Deidre was a good student as well, always receiving top grades in her elementary school. She was a serious child devoted to both her dance classes and school work. Her time for friendships was limited because of her strict ballet and school schedule. Mostly, Deidre hung out with the girls at the ballet school, who were also intensely focused on their performance and keeping their bodies rail thin.

Deidre was accepted to the Royal School of Ballet, which started in middle school. She left her family home and moved into a dorm with the other aspiring dancers. She was a brilliant student, and the other girls at school were jealous of her talent, effort, and persistence. Her ballet masters were relentless. The school allowed no time for the young dancers to have a normal social life with one another. Competition between the dancers was intensified by the rigorous routines and the pressure to perform perfectly.

Deidre developed anorexia, an eating disorder commonly found in teenagers who have rigid standards for perfection in every thing they do. Unfortunately and understandably, no one at the Royal Ballet School noticed how thin and weak this young dancer really was. Everyone thought it was just the "right look" for a ballerina.

Deidre knew just how serious her eating disorder was to her career and to her health. She reached a point where she was only eating one granola bar and one Twinkie a day, but she couldn't bring herself to eat a real meal. She suffered from malnutrition, which exacerbated the seriousness of her injury when she fell on stage and broke her foot. The doctors told her she would never be able to perform again. She was heartbroken, but not surprised.

With the end of her ballet career, this teenager suffered from a deep depression and sought out intensive psychotherapy to get her through her day-to-day life. Although she was offered admittance to an Ivy League School, she was afraid to attend because of her shyness and lack of experiences with other teenagers who were not ballerinas. Instead, she pursued an acting and modeling career because she felt comfortable as a performer. Deidre married an older, wealthy man who dominated her life much like the ballet masters of her childhood. Being in an unhappy relationship with a man such as the ballet master was a role that she was very familiar with, and she was loath to give it up.

GEOFFREY THE PIANIST

At age 18 Geoffrey was performing on a Steinway baby grand or a Yamaha upright at all of the "in" piano bars in the cosmopolitan city where he lived. He was beginning music school at a fine university with a full scholarship. Parents, friends, teachers, and mentors were sure that Geoffrey would be recognized and applauded in many noted concert halls around the world and on Broadway and in Hollywood.

Geoff started playing the piano as a child of four. His mother and grandmother were both talented musicians who rehearsed with other musicians in the family home. Musical events were as common as family dinners. This early ongoing exposure to music fed Geoffrey's love of music and talent as a pianist, composer, and creative artist. In first grade, Geoff was singled out as a child who should receive private piano lessons at school. Geoff was a part of the school band in elementary school.

Performing alone on stage and with the musical people who visited his home became normal events in his childhood and early teenage years. When Geoff was 11 he was chosen to perform a lead role in a musical comedy in a city far away from his home. He sparkled as he starred in this long musical engagement. Geoff returned to his hometown. He was accepted and given a scholarship to a fine private high school with a prestigious music department, where he performed piano solo and with choral and musical groups. He strove to be the best musician and performer among his friends, although his training was in jazz rather than classical music.

Geoff was given a full scholarship to study music at a well-known college. But the college experience became very difficult for this jazz musician, who felt held back by the constrictions of schooling and students who were more conventional learners. The pressure to compose a perfect musical work on piano at college led Geoff down the road to serious clinical depression, which often was followed by stretches of grandiosity. Geoff's musical career, both composing and performing, was interrupted and shortened.

After many years and many different types of psychotherapy, Geoff once again started to play the piano for the enjoyment of others and for his own pleasure. Piano performance is no longer a perfectionist striving. Geoff looks forward to someday finding his inspiration to compose and write songs.

Both of these highly talented individuals were driven by perfectionism in their growing years. They were never allowed to have normal childhood experiences with friends. Rather, the development of their talent was always the focus of all relationships. This exclusive focus on performance and on being the best in their field left them unable to deal with the normal everyday problems of life. Their everyday social skills were extremely inadequate. These child prodigies were limited in their ability to form meaningful emotionally satisfying relationships because they were easily bossed around and also dependent on the praise and financial support of significant others.

Parental expectations and encouragement was seriously overdetermined and overfocused. In other words, their parents lived through their children's accomplishments and genius, whether or not they were aware of it. Psychologically speaking, these parents did not allow their children to live separate emotional lives. Because their parents were so demanding, as adults these child prodigies got involved with significant others who could support them financially but dominated them emotionally. After their careers peaked, they seemed lost in the everyday world.

Avoid Underachievement: Understand Its Meaning to Your Child

Underachievement is just a label that suggests that your child is not living up to expectations, falling short of the school standards, your parental hopes, or personal expectations. Underachievement can cause grief for everyone involved. You should carefully assess the trigger for your child's underachievement.

Suppose you are an involved, attentive parent doing whatever you can, and your child is still having problems with school, and maybe at home. Perhaps there are family conflicts or unsolvable financial issues or an illness out of your control. You need to understand that it is very common for gifted children to underachieve if there is outside or internal stress in their lives. Possible causes of stress for gifted children can come from school or the home.

School stress issues can create underachievement:

- ❑ A lack of challenge or too much challenge in the classroom
- ❑ Too much competition or not enough competition
- ❑ Teacher–child personality conflicts
- ❑ A learning disability that has not been discovered or attended to
- ❑ Peer interaction problems—lack of relationships or an overly social child
- ❑ An overly structured classroom or an unstructured classroom
- ❑ No free time for creativity
- ❑ Too many expectations or not enough expectations for school work

Various home issues can create problems with underachievement:

❑ Parental arguments in front of the children

❑ Overprotectiveness and overinvolvement with the child

❑ Underinvolvement—neglect of what types of unique stimulation the child needs

❑ Too much power given to the child

❑ Sibling rivalry

❑ Pressure from parents toward perfection

❑ Illness in the family

❑ Unrealistic attitudes toward schooling

Sometimes underachievement is a normal reaction to the internal or external stresses in your child's life. First, you need to decide how serious your child's underachievement really is:

❑ *Be aware that your child is having "issues" or "problems."* Try to talk with your child about what might be going on at school and what would make her or him feel better about school, the family, friends, and so on. Talking is the first road to understanding what is out of sync with your child.

❑ *Don't be shy with your gifted child.* Ask direct questions about possible trigger points: missing homework assignments, disorganized personal belongings, excessive time on the phone or on the computer, a hostile attitude toward school friends, siblings or you, too much socializing or loneliness, and blaming others for personal problems.

❑ *Talk with your child's teachers and see what they think is the source of the problem.* Don't worry about being a pushy mother or father. It is common for teachers to doubt your child's brightness when academic problems occur. You may need to give teachers a mini-lesson on underachievement in gifted children. You can easily go online and find printable informative facts on various aspects of underachievement, which your child's teachers should become aware of so they can be your ally. If a teacher does not try to help, you have another distinct problem. Don't mash together the underachievement problem with the teacher problem; this will make the situation practically hopeless.

Remember that underachievement in gifted children is complicated. Underachievement could be brought on by stress, or it could be related to problems with your child's sense of self. Because gifted children are sensitive and introspective, they can easily blame themselves when problems with academics, talent, artistic endeavors, sports, family, or friendships surface. Blame leads to a self-defeating attitude: "I can't do it, so why try!" Or the opposite: Your child might act out anger and pain, and eventually gets in trouble at school or with the legal system.

Learn to Motivate: Bring Balance to Your Child's Life

Developing your child's unique passions is your responsibility as a parent. Understanding how to motivate your child will help you avoid the overachievement–underachievement burnout cycle. Very simply, motivation is found in the heart and in the mind. It is inspiration.

Motivation fuels your child's energy level and enthusiasm to explore and move ahead in certain areas of life. Motivation is crucial to achievement, meaningful relationships, and happiness in life. Words that are commonly associated with motivation are self-concept, self-esteem, locus of control, learned helplessness, and incentive.

Gifted children are naturally highly motivated because of their emotional intensity, persistence to complete a task, quickness, and perfectionism. Issues that gifted children have with motivation are different than the issues of nongifted children. What is most unusual is gifted children's capacity for creativity and critical thinking, which can coexist with their fear of failure and an inability to take risks.

What motivates gifted children to stick with a task may determine whether they accept the challenge and persist in the face of difficulty, or crumble or withdraw at the first sign of trouble. You can help your child persist by understanding six generalizations about motivation:

1. Intrinsic motivation is the internalized aspect of motivation—the passionate commitment to wanting to know or understand. Intrinsic motivation is necessary for any type of commitment to a personal relationship or achievement. You must nurture the intrinsic aspect of your child's interests.

2. Extrinsic motivation is the reward aspect of success. It is the applause factor, the paycheck, or the M&Ms! Extrinsic motivation is inevitable and valuable but secondary to intrinsic motivation.

3. Self-efficacy is the person's sense that they can do it—a belief in the self. You want your child to have a strong self of self-efficacy.

4. Learned helplessness is the belief that you cannot do something, no matter what. Learned helplessness is a form of negative thinking that stops your child from trying to complete a difficult task.

5. Perfectionists are vulnerable to the fear of taking a risk or the fear of failure. The best way to avoid fear of failure is to teach your child how to cope with difficult situations.

6. Teaching your child resiliency—the ability to bounce back after a disappointment—is a good way to ensure that motivation will not be an issue for your child.

"Hands On" Ways to Help Children Flourish

❑ *Encourage Your Children to Explore the World Around Them.* Gifted children are naturally highly curious. When you encourage them to explore for themselves, you are helping them find their own interests and natural talent. Exploration is an ongoing process, which is just as important to the toddler as it is to the teenager. When children are exploring, they are exposed to new ideas and see people who will help them develop their identity and teach them important life lessons.

❏ *Provide Complex and Challenging Experiences.* Give growing children all kinds of art, science, writing, and math projects that challenge their intellectual and artistic curiosity. Get them involved in real-life projects such as animal shelters or deep-sea exploration. Teenagers should be involved in community service projects. Traveling to new places and to museums will stimulate children to gain understanding into the world they live in. Later in life, these experiences may help children connect with real-world problems using their giftedness. This may help overcome the stereotype that gifted people are elitists and not involved in the real world.

❏ *Develop Verbal Capacity.* Teach your children to love books and reading. Read to your children and get their reactions. As your children learn to read on their own, discuss with them what they find interesting and important. Encourage each child to write down his or her thoughts and to express ideas.

Try to develop your children's language and vocabulary by having serious conversations with them. Introduce foreign languages as soon as your child becomes interested in them.

❏ *Develop Critical Thinking.* Ask what-if questions and listen to your child's answer. And listen to your child's own questions. Talk to your child about his or her ideas and interests with special attention to details. Work on projects that are of interest to your child and are not related to school. As children define special interests and explore them, challenge them to explain their ideas to you. This will develop creative thinking skills that can be used later in life to solve academic and real life issues.

❑ *Pay Attention to Your Child's Creative Side.* Provide a safe and loving home environment where your child can feel safe expressing him- or herself. Gifted children enjoy looking at different ways to solve a problem. Encourage divergent thinking. Expose them to art projects and art classes. Expose them to music, dance, and the movies, and provide lessons in the areas of greatest interest. Take them to concerts and museums to show them where originality and aesthetics flourish. Creativity can also be facilitated by responding to all types of questions.

❑ *Support Healthy Risk Taking.* Encourage risk taking by rewarding good efforts as well as good accomplishment. Research shows that the avoidance of risk, or the inability or unwillingness to take risks when opportunities present themselves, interferes with high achievement, contributes to underachievement, and interferes with the attainment of high leadership and life satisfaction. Some gifted children definitely are very afraid to try anything new out of fear of failure, which is coupled with their own perfectionist expectations.

For example, you could encourage your child to take a chance by participating yourself in an unfamiliar special-interest class. Show your child how you take chances in your own life. Discuss with your child what you learn from just trying something new.

❑ *Praise Your Children.* Praise is essential. Praise develops self-esteem and self-confidence. Praise from adults helps children and teenagers tone down their self-critical nature, perfectionism, and unreachably sky-high expectations.

❑ *Allow for Setbacks.* When children are working on something new, they sometimes revert back to an early stage of development. Parents need to understand that gifted children are not gifted all of the time. Have realistic expectations for your child. Too much pressure on gifted children can harm their self-esteem and self-confidence.

❏ *Balance Social Life with School Life.* Every day children need to be involved in nonacademic activities such as music, free play, dance, or sports to help to relieve stress and to expose them to different aspects of life. Too much focus on one aspect of life will create long-range problems.

❏ *Gifted Children Need Mentors.* Find tutors or other adults who can encourage and help develop your child's talents and interests. This will take some pressure off of you and their teachers to provide all of the stimulation that gifted children need. Biographies of gifted adults teach us that most of the successfully gifted had mentors who helped them develop.

❏ *Do Not Ignore Your Child's Uniqueness.* Talk to your child about how he or she feels about being especially talented or advanced in certain areas of life. Get your child's feelings and opinions. You will be very surprised to hear your son or daughter talk about what it is like to be gifted. For example, a five-year-old highly gifted child told me that he knew he was smarter than the other children at school. He said, "The most popular kids are not that smart. I don't let other kids know how smart I am. I wouldn't be a part of the group."

❏ *Make School Meaningful.* Smart children need to actually understand the importance of school. It is not good enough to tell your child that school is something every child has to do. Smart kids are curious enough to ask why. Try to show your child why school work is meaningful if it is not immediately interesting. When you work with your child on projects, basic skills, or homework, try to reinforce how the task is relevant to everyday life and to the future.

❏ *Teach the Importance of Effort.* Gifted children are very quick learners. Still, they need to learn the importance of trying when work is tough or when work is boring. One way to teach your child what it means to make an effort is to point out the success a child is making in a particular subject, project, or in an area of talent such as math, reading, spelling, or piano. Teach your child to assess his or her skills and to gain confidence in accomplishments. Give your child feedback about success and help with challenges.

❑ *Teach Children to Listen to Their Inner Drummer.* Make sure that your child is internally or intrinsically invested in the activities he or she participates in, as this will avoid problems with overachievement and underachievement.

Teach your children through your own behavior that it is not always important to be the best. Being passionately involved is far more important.

What Parents Have to Say About Gifted Potential

> *"Kids are born with giftedness, and it's the parents' responsibility (and hopefully their desire!) to provide the opportunities and outlets to help their child develop to his or her full potential. The parents also need to help the child become a well-rounded person. Kids benefit from exposure to a range of viewpoints, experiences, physical activities, and environments. A child that excels in math, for example, should be encouraged to explore other areas, just as athletes cross-train and colleges require course work in a breadth of areas."*
> Angela

> *"Well . . . Jake has a high IQ, brilliant aptitude in science and math, but major motor sensory integration disorder. Case in point, he completed intense math and reading homework complete with writing sentences, but when he was in the shower, I asked him to bend over and wash his toes and he couldn't make his body do this action, so gifted is a bit subjective to me. A 'normal' well rounded child with average aptitude would have been a gifted child to me at certain times with issues I face with my precious Jake. Jake will do anything a 'smart' child does but will not participate in anything a*

'normal' child would do because he may look stupid. 'Normal' kids don't worry about looking stupid.

"So the upshot is, I am going to force this issue with Jake. He is seven, and he must develop his motor skills no matter how stupid he looks. I am going to the mat on this—probably I'll have to bribe him. But it will be worth it." Mary

"Born gifted. I always say, 'He came fully himself—outgoing, curious, with a sense of humor, very loving—innate, yes.' I need to get him into theatrical training as he has such a penchant for mimicry, characterization, and humorous delivery. Giftedness is there; it came with the child.

"You as a parent need to keep your eyes and ears open and to keep the child going forward. Give him exposure and opportunities in his area of interest. At first allow him his own development. Then as he gets older, say, by six, in a more structured environment that is not too limiting, you have to help him with thoughtful opportunity. It is not easy." Trish

"Rachel was definitely born with her potential. She knew what she wanted before she could talk. Beginning when she was a few months old, she would look people straight in the eye and strangers would go out of their way to comment, usually searching for the appropriate way to express it and eventually saying, 'She's so focused.' I actually stopped taking her to the supermarket." Tanya

"I definitely believe that he came to us with certain gifts. I am not taking credit for his brilliance. But it does not hurt that we have books in the house and outside enrichment. We travel and visit museums as a family. Our son is involved in sports and takes piano lessons.

"We did not push him to read and to write. He wanted to learn. It was meant to be." Cynthia

Nurturing Your Child's Potential

Try your very best to find out what your child is especially talented at and then help him or her learn to really love this part of themselves. Teach your child the importance of passion for an interest, idea, or project. Be very careful not to promote a certain type of achievement or talent to please you and your family, the teachers, or to get ahead. Focusing on external rewards too often backfires into underachievement and easy burnout, as already described.

Remember that challenging your child is very different from pushing your child. Gifted children definitely need to be stimulated if they are going to soar. You should be your child's advocate, not talent agent or business manager.

Questions to Ask Yourself

1. Do I know my child's learning strengths and challenges?
2. How do I nurture my child?
3. Is my child underachieving? Why or why not?
4. Can my child listen to his or her inner voice?
5. Is my child happy most of the time?
6. What are my child's passions?
7. How do I show my child that being the best is only one part of achievement?

Family Issues in the Life of the Gifted Child

"Parenting gifted children takes extra attention to certain family issues and dynamics. Sensitivity really needs to be anticipated and appropriately recognized, and emotional responses should not be discredited (and never, ever, ridiculed, as we see all too often these days). My most sensitive child is also the sibling least comfortable expressing that sensitivity. A casual observer will often think he has thick skin and will not recognize his vulnerability. As a parent, you never want to react like a casual observer, and you want to educate the 'casual observers' when appropriate, particularly if that person is a teacher.

"If one sibling is more sensitive or emotional, you need to be careful not to label this personality trait as better or worse. And regardless of IQ, all siblings need abundant feedback for their talents, achievements, capacity for empathy, and whatever else makes them special people."
                                                                    Angela

Caring for a family is an incredibly important responsibility that most parents take on somewhat idealistically and innocently. Inevitably, normal issues or problems arise that need to be understood and negotiated, no matter how thoughtful, patient, enlightened, or financially stable you try to be with your children. As the parent of a gifted child, you have "smart children" family issues to deal with in addition to normal family life issues.

Retrospective life histories of notable gifted individuals indicate the importance of a balanced family structure, of having confidence in your child, and of a belief or vision about what is essential in parenting. In contrast, parents who live through their child's accomplishments at the expense of nurturing the whole child seem to be the most ineffective and destructive parents, based on my experiences working with families with gifted children.

Strive for Balance

Finding balance in the family is crucial if vital family relationships are to be established and nurtured. Balance will evolve if each family member is treated as an individual and given the respect each deserves. Just as you have to learn to listen to and value your children, the reverse is also true. Your children need to learn to appreciate your efforts and feel the true give and take of communication. This type of balance in a family will take time, lots of effort, and thoughtfulness. Snap judgments and quick actions will undermine family balance.

The first step in developing balance in your family life involves seeing each member of the family as a whole person and a unique individual. This means you should *not* label your child as *the gifted one* or *the genius*. Attaching a label to a child might seem harmless, but this type of imposed identity is a dangerous and destructive way of relating to your very smart child. Sharing your personal perceptions with your child and with others will limit your child's overall social and emotional development and create an unhealthy pressure to excel. Labeling a child creates distance between you and your child, as well as between your child and others.

Favoritism is another type of labeling that creates dysfunction and imbalance in a family. There is no excuse not to treat each family member as special, lovable, worthy of your time, and valuable. The demands of the exceedingly bright child may make you believe that he or she needs all of your attention. However, limits need to be established for the highly curious child. Try to be aware of how that child's demands affect other family members. Make sure not to spend all of your time with your most intense child. Talk to your kids about how they have to share mom and dad's time.

If you believe that your oldest is a little smarter or a lot smarter than your middle child or younger child, keep this information to yourself. If you feel like spreading the word, try to understand where these feelings and thoughts that you have to show off to others are coming from. You might ask yourself, "Why am I using my child to improve my self-esteem?" "Does my older child remind me of someone in my past who was extremely smart?" To keep yourself grounded, ask yourself, "What notable qualities *and* problems does my smart child possess?"

Labeling one child as *superior,* another sibling as the *caretaker,* and the youngest as the *slow* child will create lifelong problems for the entire family. Let's look at a troubling case history where the children in one family were divided into genius and nongenius categories. This case history clearly illustrates the problems created by labeling children. It also illustrates other common problems that families with gifted children contend with, which include the following:

❑ The destructiveness of labeling a child as gifted

❑ Overfocus on the child's strengths and neglect of the child's weaknesses

❑ Overidentification with the labeled child's accomplishments

- ❑ Rejection of the parents and rejection or resentment of the gifted child by nongifted siblings

- ❑ Empowerment of the idealized child with adult authority and decision making

- ❑ Discipline of overly powerful gifted children

- ❑ Lowered self-esteem of children who are treated as second in line

- ❑ Power struggles in the family

"OUR SON, THE GENIUS"—THE MARKOWITZ FAMILY

Steven, the oldest son of educated middle-class Jewish parents, was given the label of *genius* in his early childhood because he was very curious and quick, an early reader, and a math wiz. Sam and Sophie Markowitz were not the richest people in the family, but they could show off their smart son to their competitive relatives. They loved to brag about their son's giftedness to friends, neighbors, teachers, and to their large extended family. Achievement and success were highly coveted by Sam and Sophie and their Jewish community. The sense of competitiveness about being "the best" in the extended family was transmitted to Steve, who was pitted against his seriously aggressive cousins. Eventually, Steve was known as the smartest child in the synagogue, alongside his most artistic and musical cousins and his rich aunts and uncles.

As each year passed, Sophie became more aware and concerned that Steve was very spoiled—demanding, lonely, and socially awkward. Giving Steve a brother or sister was Sophie's simplistic solution to making her son a more normal child in a social sense. Steve was six years old when his sister Rebecca was born. Following closely was Nancy, who was one year younger than her sister.

The addition of two children was almost too much for Steve to emotionally handle. After six years, he was no longer the center of attention. This young boy was angry at his parents that his life was now more complicated and chaotic. Equally painful was Steve's jealousy of his sisters, who received a lot of attention from grandparents, aunts, uncles, friends, and neighbors. Steve became unmanageable. He was always out of control unless he was working on a scientific experiment with his friends or being the boss of his younger sisters.

To cut down on family scenes and arguments, Sam and Sophie moved to a bigger house, with the hope that making more space for everyone would bring harmony to their home life. Still, Steve remained a know-it-all who had difficulty tolerating or accepting his sisters' needs for attention. Even as young children, Rebecca and Nancy learned that they were second best. They learned to listen to their older brother as they picked up that their mother was allowing him to be in charge of the family.

As the years passed, Sam withdrew more and more from his parental role. He resented his son's smartness and his potential to become the doctor Sam had wanted to be. The energy it took Sophie to educate Steve made Sam jealous. Sam indeed knew that his son was a lot smarter than he was. He felt threatened that Steve could solve very difficult scientific and mathematical problems. Sam felt and was treated as if he were second best to his son. A deep bitterness developed between these parents, as well as a deep schism in the family. Sam's resentment eventually turned into rejection of his son.

Sophie was a very gifted woman, and she was not threatened by her son. Actually, she was *overly* proud of him. Sophie, having made her son a know-it-all monster, seemed to have no choice but to put him in charge as the pseudo father of her daughters. As a teenager, Steve helped Sophie make decisions about family issues. Although he was indeed exceptionally rational, he lacked the wisdom that one can only gain from life experiences. The entire family was out of balance. Reliable parental decision making was almost unavailable, as Sophie and Sam could not agree on any issue. In short, the house was chaotic.

Nancy and Rebecca kept to themselves and tried to do well at school. The sisters listened to their older brother, knowing that he had the power to okay friends, clothes, their higher education, and even when they could get their driver's licenses. Although they were both very bright and talented, they knew and accepted that they had to live in their brother's shadow. Nancy and Rebecca never received the encouragement and self-confidence that they needed and longed for to become as accomplished as their brother, the genius. And so they did as they were told until they left home.

The genius label left Steve a lonely child and adolescent. As an adult, Steve made friendships with other scientists in his field, and he eventually married a talented engineer who shared his knowledge and passion for his work. In his field of scientific inquiry, Steve was considered a true genius. His stellar research was the best in the world. But Steve remained extremely awkward with anybody who did not understand his genius. His adulthood was very focused and limited to certain scientific interests that required extensive travel around the world. Steve remained detached from any nuclear family functions, although he did manage to find the time to attend his parents' funerals.

Rebecca and Nancy left home for college and forged their own paths. Both sisters were insecure and competitive with one another, which intensified their quests for high achievement. As adults they were not close to one another, and they had rather limited contact with Sam, Sophie, and Steve. Although they were seriously insecure about who they were when they got out of their brother's shadow, over time they managed to develop and pursue their own personal and intellectual interests.

Both women married and had families and successful careers. However, each sister suffered from deep emotional conflict and pain because her self-worth had been seriously undermined in the developmental years. Unlike their brother Steve, friendships and a variety of interests filled their lives. But finding comfort with one another had not been sanctioned by their parents and did not thrive in their adulthood.

The troubled life story of the Markowitz family is an all-too-common one when parents live through their child and are not armed with enough knowledge about how to raise a gifted child. The traps that these parents fell into are unforgivable—but almost understandable, given the challenges, intensity, argumentativeness, and perfectionism of the extremely bright child. Let's break down the "mistakes" in parenting that were made by Mr. and Mrs. Markowitz:

1. Labeling a child as a genius is extremely destructive to the child's developing sense of self and to the normal unfolding of family life. Understanding how smart your child really is and then working with his or her strengths and weaknesses is a far cry from parading your child around as a genius. Attaching a label to a child arrests overall development because it puts a limitation on social and emotional growth. If taken to the extreme, labeling your child is a form of emotional child abuse that has longstanding psychological ramifications.

2. Overfocusing on the child's strengths and ignoring weaknesses creates an individual who will be out of balance in life. Announcing to yourself and your spouse and community that you are *aware* that your child is socially awkward is *not* enough. In order to solve your child's problems interacting with others, you must be proactive and work directly with your child to develop social interaction skills. Families should also elicit the support of the classroom teacher and the significant caregivers, so that the awkward child does not become isolated. Socialization skills can be taught and mastered.

3. Overidentifying with your child's talents creates unrealistic and confused expectations for each individual in the family and the well-being of the family unit. Overidentifying with a child creates confusion about who is doing what for whom. When a parent is overidentified, there is psychological confusion about the parent–child roles. In a healthy family, the parents are the caregivers, and they are not entitled to elicit narcissistic rewards for the child's accomplishments. By *narcissistic rewards,* I mean having an inflated sense of importance because your child is talented, and using the child's accomplishments to feel better about yourself as a parent and as a person. While it is normal for parents to get joy from their children's talents, it is not normal and is really unhealthy and emotionally destructive for parents to use their children to feel better about themselves. Some parents can actually live through their children and not have their own lives and life goals. This role con-

fusion is a burden for the child and creates an imbalance in the family. It is a seriously big parenting mistake.

4. Resentment or rejection of the gifted child by a nongifted parent can create a disastrous environment for everyone. This consequence can be avoided if every member of the family is considered integral to the well-being of the family unit. Favoring or overvaluing extreme intelligence is destructive because it can lead to serious resentments and deep splits in a family.

5. Empowering the idealized child with adult decision making is an abdication of the parental role, which can create a child with antisocial personality disorder and a highly unbalanced, dysfunctional family. When parents delegate their responsibility and roles to their children, serious parenting mistakes follow. Although gifted children may be able to make adult decisions, they lack the judgment and wisdom that comes with life experiences. As well, making adult decisions will burden the gifted child and rob him or her of a childhood. This leads the child to deeply resent the parents. Obviously, unexpressed resentments between parent and child undermine a cohesive family life and breed anger and hate.

6. Disciplining gifted children who have an inflated sense of themselves is very difficult, if not impossible. When parents have extreme difficulty with their smart child acting as just another responsible member of the family, there is reason to believe that the child has too much power. Gifted children need to understand and follow the limits imposed upon them by their parents and teachers. As well, family life rules need to be respected and valued. Every child in a family is valuable and worthy of an equal say in their family life. A child who cannot respect the family rules needs help from a professional mental health provider.

7. All siblings in a family should be treated with respect, encouragement, and love. It is always a mistake to favor one child over the other children. Having a favorite child leads to having children who, by default, are second best. Self-esteem and the devel-

opment of the child's individual strengths are undermined when one child is singled out as the best and the others are ignored.

8. Power struggles develop in a family when parents have too many unrealistic expectations for their smart child. Usually parents do not know what is reasonable to expect from their extremely talented child. When you are educated about characteristics of gifted children, you will avoid power struggles because you will know when to back off and when to set realistic limits that promote discipline. As one parent, Mary, said in Chapter 6, there are some issues on which you have to "go to the mat"—you have to win those. Other issues might not be so important. You might have to pick your battles, but you must be willing to stay in the fight and win the battles you pick.

Normal Gifted Family Issues

Families with gifted children will have unique problems to contend with that grow out of their child's intense curiosity and emotionality. Sam and Sophie Markowitz had absolutely no insight into their own parenting enactments or mistakes, and they were not educated about how to raise an extremely precocious child. Consequently, serious family problems developed that fragmented family bonds and inhibited the development of each child's overall potential. This worst-case scenario and other harmful situations can be prevented if you pay careful attention to each individual in the family. You should think about how you are handling the following issues.

Showing Favoritism

Struggles over favoritism can be more difficult and intense in families with gifted children, for many reasons. Gifted children are often energetic and emotionally intense, and they naturally demand a lot of attention from their parents. In addition, some gifted children are insecure because of their emotional intensity. Such children might want to be favored, but you cannot spend all of your energy on your gifted child. To raise healthy children, you have to treat all children in the family as unique and valuable in their own right.

When the family structure is in and of itself valued and respected by all, then there is little chance that favoritism will become an issue or get out of control. Cooperation between siblings and parents should also be a high priority. I have worked with many families who are respectful of one another, and they do not have conflicts over who is more loved.

Establish Rules That Make Sense and Can Be Followed

Gifted children can be demanding, emotional, relentless, untiring, and persistent. They move to the beat of their own drummer. Biographies of gifted adults show us that very bright children are frequently difficult to raise, and they often have turbulent childhoods. But you must make sure your smart kids learn to follow the family rules and regulations. When gifted kids make up the rules, the family structure becomes unbalanced and dysfunctional.

You need to be careful to establish rules that your gifted children can follow. Strict standards and too many expectations for children are as inappropriate as a lack of order and no expectations. When you value family cooperation alongside the development of each family member, you will be able to set up realistic rules that will be meaningful to all concerned.

Power struggles over right and wrong and following the rules can, to some extent, be attributed to the wrong rules and expectations. If you understand the unique characteristics of gifted children and integrate these attributes into your child-rearing strategies, you will have less difficulty with your children following the rules. Accept that your child will, at some point, become frustrated. Frustration is necessary to develop self-discipline.

Learn How to Motivate Your Child

You need to learn the art of motivation if you are going to have any success with getting your bright child to follow the house rules. "I don't care what you say, I am not going to listen to you," is a common refrain. Figuring out how to make your child care about what you are saying is a challenge for any parent, whether the child is gifted or not.

When you are as honest as possible with your child about your own expectations, you might have the upper hand when you are giving directions. In some situations, it will seem like nothing works. Your child simply refuses to listen to you. Promising a trip to the moon will not make your child budge. At these times when your frustration and your child's frustration are high, it helps to have some understanding of how to connect and calm your child down. Understanding what motivates your child will help you to get your point across.

You can easily learn to connect with your child effectively when she is in problem-free areas. Using this knowledge about the most effective way to relate to your child is enormously useful when your child is really stressed out and feeling defeated. Read Chapter 5 to understand strategies that facilitate communication.

Creating deliberately paced challenges will motivate your child to achieve at his or her own pace, as well as to learn how to deal with frustration. Gifted children need to learn to take risks and to learn that the price of success is hard work.

Your Child's Argumentativeness Needs an Outlet— Not a Family Takeover

Often, families with gifted children have issues with children being argumentative and bossy. This stems from certain characteristics of gifted children: They are bright, curious, verbal, introspective, intense, focused, and persistent. You need to find outlets for your children's debating nature—for example, debate teams, chess competitions, and theatrical groups. Leadership roles at school and community service projects allow your child to voice his or her opinion in an acceptable forum where success is a predictable outcome.

In contrast, long, drawn-out arguments between parents and children, between sister and brother, and between student and teacher are at best a waste of energy for everyone involved. At worst, bossiness and argumentativeness can arouse anger, hurt feelings, and diminish self-esteem and self-confidence for everyone involved. So you will have to set clear guidelines that your child can follow. These will help you, as well, to know when to allow your child to speak up, and when to calmly make it clear that your child's argumentative behavior is unnecessary and hurtful.

Emotional Intensity Needs to Be Channeled and Contended with Appropriately

Bright children can be emotional, and their moodiness or heightened sensitivity will affect family life. Emotional quickness, like intellectual quickness, can be disarming for those in the receiving line of fire. A child or teenager with strong and changing emotional states can be exhausting. Parents need to work together to find a way to fit their child's emotional intensity into the functioning of the family.

Developing goals and expectations for a cohesive emotional life is important. When your child can attend to, and hopefully, respect other people's sensitivity, you will have accomplished an important cornerstone to a balanced family. In other words, when all family members can express their point of view without humiliation or fear of retribution, emotional balance in the family is more likely.

Sibling Rivalry Is Normal

Parents can make competition between talented children pathological and destructive by overvaluing their achievements and encouraging competition. You have to learn to accept that your children will naturally evaluate one another and will sometimes fight with each other. Overreacting, or mentally writing differences between children in stone, intensifies the natural competition between children. Siblings will develop better long-term relationships with one another if cooperation is valued over competition. When sibling rivalry is a continual issue, each sister or brother probably needs individual attention from their parents.

When one child is favored because he or she is gifted, then everyone in the family suffers, as I pointed out at the beginning of the chapter. Often, the favored child is given too much adult power and uses this power against his or her siblings. When siblings are abusive to one another, families will eventually become fractured and alienation is the only possible outcome.

Don't Oversell or Undersell Your Child to Others

Dealing with the neighbors or relatives who want to gawk at your child because he or she is so smart or talented is really a big problem. Children need to be protected from onlookers who make them feel odd, different, weird, or like the neighborhood nerd. Your awareness that this might happen is the first step in learning to protect your child.

Being in denial or pretending that your child is not smart is certainly not a solution. Finding a comfortable way to deal with intrusive questions or reactions will take some sensitivity and creativity on your part. There are no easy answers to this family issue, which can become very problematic when ignored. Chapter 1 addresses the issues that parents in denial confront as their child gets older.

Avoid Family Arguments That Require Children to Take Sides

When parents disagree or see a parenting issue quite differently, gifted children can pick this up very easily. They are able to play one parent against the other to their ostensible advantage. These unhealthy alliances can create long-range misunderstandings, which become disastrous for everyone involved, because the gifted child is being treated as an adult with a great deal of authority in the family. Always remember that your gifted child is a *child,* no matter how smart he or she is, and should not be given the power of being your confidant or friend. It may be hard to stop your child from taking sides or acting like your buddy. However, it pays off to try to keep your child as a child—the result will be a well adjusted child, better equipped for adulthood when the time comes.

When there are marital problems and the gifted child has too much adult power, then there is an even more serious issue, which may require help from a mental heath professional. There are instances where the child can become an ally with one parent over the other. In pre-divorce situations the child who becomes a parental ally is denied the security of having two parents who can provide love and nurturing. This loss of parental love may create an emotional injury that is very difficult to repair. Using your gifted child to act out your anger at your spouse is a form of child abuse that is difficult to repair, even with a great deal of intensive psychotherapy.

Accept That Very Bright Children Can Have Difficulties in Social Situations

A child who is in the top 98 or 99 percent in his area of talent or intellectual capacity is going to fit into a social group very differently than an average child, a high-ability child, or a child with disabilities. When you or other family members have unrealistic goals for normality from such a child, everyone will be disappointed. Family conflicts over appropriate social interaction can be avoided if and when you accept that your bright child is probably not going to be in the most popular crowd. Most likely, a gifted child will fit in with the smart kids who are interested in more mature areas of similar interests than their same-age peer group.

Don't Excuse Inappropriate Social Misbehavior

When parents excuse their child's inappropriate or unacceptable behavior because they are quirky and gifted, then real problems for the family develop. In other words, don't sanction your child's clever or strange behavior because he or she is gifted. Try to understand why your child is cleverly misbehaving, and try as hard as you can to put a stop to it.

I remember six-year-old Jacob, who was very angry and frustrated with his parents and his brother. Jacob would make bombs out of baby powder and try and blow up his bedroom. His parents thought that he was just being clever. I thought that Jacob's parents should help him to explore and understand what was making him so angry. But they dismissed my suggestions and remained amused. Consequently, Jacob had problems with his anger that affected his school achievement. Instead of talking with a therapist, he acted out his oppositional behavior with teachers and other authority figures.

Unfortunately, parents often cherish their child's giftedness but do not offer discipline or guidance, which results in a child who is rude and self-absorbed and overly entitled. Even though gifted children believe deeply that they know it all, they need to be taught limits and social graces.

Don't Overidentify with Your Child

I have pointed out the hazards of overidentification in almost every chapter because it is a crucial issue that you as a parent have some control over. Although you can't choose your child's peers or find the perfect school, you *can* control how you relate to your child.

Overidentification is a broad psychological term. For parents, overidentification means overreacting to your child's demands and accomplishments because of an overinvestment in the child. Overidentification is the opposite of being cold, distant, and unavailable. The overreactive parent is *too* concerned with the child's development. Overeager parents are too sensitive and too available because they have their own motives. For example, no amount of time or money is too much for the mother who is living through her child's artistic ability or intelligence. Or, any behavior is OK when dad wants his son to be a great scientist or soccer player or musician. When parents are overidentified, they are giving and wanting to get more than they should from their child.

I have spent countless hours with my gifted mothers parenting groups talking about different aspects of overidentification. I asked my group members to write about what they know about overidentification. Here is what they had to say:

> "Overidentifying with your child can be an inadequacy on the part of the parents who did not accomplish what they set out to do for themselves. That is why I was a parent at a later age. I achieved my career aspirations. Having children was an extra blessing. I see both my children as very unique and individual. I see them as separate and apart from myself. My daughter and son are not an extension of me. They are their own separate beings. When one child or the other is upset, I get upset for them but I don't make it my own issue, because it is not. This allows my children freedom to be their own person."   Linda

> "We want so much for our children. We often project our hopes and dreams onto them. I do hope my children are happy and that they reach their potential. Sometimes we are too sensitive to their needs and wants because of our own need to be perfect. So-called perfect parents want perfect children. When we see them not reaching the bar we set for them emotionally, intellectually, and socially, we freak

out and think there is a problem that we can fix. The problem
usually doesn't exist.

"Overidentification is when the child coughs and the mother
takes the cough drop. I try to avoid over-doing by not hovering over my
children. I don't analyze every aspect of their behavior. I don't look at
them under the microscope. I look at the whole child. I try to let them
make their own mistakes and learn from them."   Isabelle

"Overidentification? Guilty as charged. I was 36 when Luke was born
and couldn't wait to trade in my career to be with this amazing little
baby boy. I realize that I've approached it with a singlemindedness
that has been both a curse and a blessing. I do believe the hours and
hours we played with blocks and read books and walked in endless
loops around the neighborhood have all contributed positively to his
development. He is a thoughtful, sweet child who was reading at two-
and-a-half and doing math by three. On the downside, however, I also
taught Luke to expect that he could have my attention whenever he
wanted it. And that he could have a say in many of the decisions
about where we go and what we play. In some ways I treat him a little
bit like a guest. And as crazy as that sounds, it never seemed that
crazy to me. After all, what could possibly be more important than
raising Luke? Fortunately, I'm beginning to understand that you don't
do your children any favors when you try to remove all the obstacles in
their path. Boredom, in particular, is a good teacher, and I wish I'd let
Luke work his way out of it from time to time instead of always
making myself so available to him. It's tough not to put your child at
the center of the world when you've waited so long for him and love
him so dearly, but clearly it's not good for anyone to believe that
they're the center of the universe."   Laura

"There are two pitfalls and one possible advantage associated with
overidentification. The first pitfall is seen in many Westside LA
parents—they try to live through their children. They want their
children to be achievers in sports, music, or academics. It is not fair
to expect a child to achieve to make his parents happy.

"The second pitfall is that when something happens that is
upsetting to your child, it upsets you as well, more than it ought to.
Often this is because the upsetting event reminds you of things that
happened to you as a child. Then your own child senses that you are

*very upset, and gets even more upset than he was to begin with.
Don't make a bad situation worse by projecting your own feelings
onto it.*

*"The good thing—the possible advantage—to overidentification
is that it may go hand-in-hand with an ability to identify with your
child in a healthy way, which is very useful. Gifted parents often
understand their children better than teachers, coaches, and other
nongifted adults. Parents often get bad advice from others who can't
identify with a gifted child. For example, I know my older son needs
an unusually high degree of autonomy for a 12-year-old. I know this
in part because I remember how hard it was for me to be a passive
recipient of learning, and I see this in my son as well. Not all his
teachers see this, and some perceive his desire for autonomy as
resistance. Yet a gifted child like my son is often 'older' than their
stated age and more than ready for independence."*   Janice

*"Overidentification can be detrimental to both the child and the
parent. Parents need to be careful about making their personal
issues into issues for their kids. My advice is to be very careful about
what you verbally dwell on with a child regarding disappointments,
favoritism, etc., since you can pass 'issues' down to kids. A parent
who overidentifies with his child's baseball strike-out can lead the
child to believe that such incidents are disappointing instead of just
part of a fun game."*   Angela

*"I tend to overidentify with my son's emotional struggles. I sometimes
remember similar situations in my childhood and re-experience the
pain. Oftentimes, I feel responsible, somehow, for not adequately
diverting the pain makers or being able to help enough when
pertaining to a situation brought on by adults. Perhaps my inclination
is somehow connected to my childhood, bringing up feelings of
helplessness in me.*

*"What I do know is this. I love my child more than anything and
we are connected in an organic way as well. He and I sense each
other's beats."*   Tony

*"Because my son is gifted and has motor sensory integration disorder
I think I over-observe and overfocus. It's hard for me to identify
with Jake because he's a male and I have different issues. I am*

overprotective and a little too hovering. I work very hard at pulling back on this.

"To me Jake is perfect. I love him and he's just perfect. I could care less about whether or not he is mainstream or popular. I worry about him getting asthma and feeling like he is uncoordinated or 'not cool,' as he puts it. Some kids told him he wants to be cool because he is not good at sports.

"Our divorce causes me to overnurture and hover even more."

Mary

"I worry about my son. I identify with him because I have empathy for him. Sometimes I have too much empathy and other times not enough.

"I seek to protect George. I fear his being hurt or feeling rejected or left out. I wonder, is this projection on my part or overidentification?"

Trish

Hold on Tightly to Your Own Life

Parents who are too involved with their children's lives often have not lived out their own dreams, have unhappy marriages, or are single parents. Overinvolvement with the gifted child can also be observed in parents who are too focused on their child's achievements and/or talents. Parents who want to give their child what they did not get in their own childhood often are overfocused or psychologically enmeshed with their child. Giving to your child what you did not get can include indulgence or spoiling your child. You will be much better off living your own life—and so will your children.

Related to this issue of parental overinvolvement is the reality that gifted children need their parents to be their advocates. Getting a gifted child the appropriate type of education may require you to spend an enormous amount of time and energy. Research shows that successful gifted individuals have had parents who were very involved and capable of developing their child's potential. There is a fine line between being a pushy, enmeshed parent and being your child's advocate. Hopefully, you will be able to make this distinction.

When to Look for Help from a Professional

It is a very personal decision to seek out the help of a mental health professional. Most parents consider a psychological evaluation or psychotherapy when other options do not seem to be helpful enough. Avenues you should consider before talking to a psychologist or counselor trained in the characteristic problems of the gifted are as follows:

1. Seek out a support group that is made up of other parents with gifted children.
2. Talk to all of the teachers at your child's school who might have insight into your child's problems.
3. Read about problems of gifted children or go online and see what professionals have to say.
4. Attend meetings in your area about your parenting concerns.
5. Speak with your child's pediatrician about your developmental concerns.
6. Consider having your own psychotherapy to gain insight into what you might unknowingly bring to your child's developmental issues. For example, if you were verbally abused as a child you might have problems expressing anger and setting appropriate limits for your son or daughter.

When you find yourself with an emotional problem related to your child or your parenting that you can't get a handle on, you need to seek out professional help. It is always better to be too cautious than to ignore problems. Actually, you have nothing to lose when you seek out advice, support, or some type of psychotherapy.

One to three consultation hours may really help you or your child feel better about what is troubling him or her. If more time is required to solve a family or child development problem, it is important for you not to view this type of intervention as your failure. Rather, when you seek out help and have a positive attitude, you will teach your children that asking for help is an important part of learning how to cope with life and the development of one's potential. Parents who see asking for help as shameful will teach their children to withdraw into themselves or to act out their problems in unacceptable ways.

Final Thoughts—Instant Advice on Handling Family Issues

Educated and insightful parents will be better able to handle the unique smart family problems that they have to cope with. Being a thoughtful and understanding parent is crucial as you try to be a good enough parent. Finding other adults who can support you in your decision making is critical. Being ready to set limits when necessary will help you develop a family structure that is in balance.

Questions to Consider

1. Think about how your family of origin worked together. Did your mother have a favorite child? Why do mothers choose favorites?

2. Do you have the same goals for family life as your parents did? How do your goals differ, and why?

3. Did your mother overidentify with some children and not the others?

4. Do you overidentify with your children? If so, why?

5. How do you react to others who treat differently or mistreat your child because he/she is gifted?

6. Do you try to maintain a lively relationship with your spouse outside of parenting?

7. Who do you turn to for advice on parenting?

8. Do you feel like you could turn to a mental health professional if you are having problems with your child? Why or why not?

9. Do you know how to motivate your child?

CHAPTER EIGHT

Ten Key Rules for Raising Productive and Well-Adjusted Gifted Children

The ten rules presented in this chapter will provide you with a set of important guidelines for how to interact successfully with your gifted child. If you've read the previous chapters, you will understand why the following rules are so very important. If you started with this chapter, maybe these rules will inspire you to go to the beginning of the book.

Rule 1: A little understanding goes a long way. A great deal of understanding will make you an effective parent.

This rule sounds simple, but actually it is very complicated to understand and follow. That's because there are at least three components involved in the understanding process:

1. *Understanding your child's unique strengths and learning challenges*. This understanding can be accomplished through a formal psychological evaluation.

   Or this understanding may be accomplished by detailed observations, school reports, or talent reports.

2. *Understanding what it means to you as a parent to have a gifted child*. Are you proud, shocked, overwhelmed, or concerned about how to deal with your own reactions to your child? Don't live through your child. See Chapter 1 to understand this point in more detail.

3. *Understanding the behavioral characteristics of gifted children*. Respect what is unique about your child. Chapter 4 explains the most common behavioral characteristics of gifted children.

Rule 2: It is better to be a "good enough" parent than a perfect parent to your gifted child.

Parents today are more savvy about raising healthy, productive children. There is a broad range of popular books available on how to parent. Hopefully, abuse and neglect of children and teenagers is on a downward trend.

Ironically, as the development and education of children and adolescents has become an investment in the future, some parents have made parenting into a full-time career. Overfocus on parenting that creates anxiety in both the child and parents is counterproductive. The popular psychology term for mothers and fathers who hover over their children is *helicopter parents*.

Gifted children are highly sensitive and perfectionist by nature. If you try to be perfect, you will intensify the anxiety in your children. If you understand how to be a good-enough parent, you will be more effective. See Chapter 2 for an extensive explanation of how to parent a gifted child.

Rule 3: You must deal with the reality that gifted children are emotionally intense, which leads to moodiness and bossy behavior.

You should empathize with your child's intense feelings, but not necessarily give in to their demands for action. Learning to communicate with your gifted child is a challenge. By learning how to react appropriately and set fair limits, you will be better able to live through and enjoy the experience of parenting a gifted child. Chapter 5 deals with how to deal with your know-it-all child.

Rule 4: Understand the school options for your child, and select the best school you can find. Keep in mind there is no perfect school.

This is a serious challenge that can take up a lot of your parental time and energy. Educating a gifted child is more difficult than educating a child with average or even superior intellectual abilities. You will be better prepared to make the best decision regarding schooling if you are knowledgeable about the specific needs of gifted children. Chapter 3 addresses this issue in detail.

Rule 5: Learn how to be your child's advocate.

As the parent of a gifted child, you need to make other people who work with your child aware of his or her potential. You will actually have to become an advocate for your child's giftedness—be it intellectual, emotional, social, mathematical, musical, or artistic.

Advocating for your child does not mean pushing your child. You need to understand the difference between a child who is being challenged at the optimal level and a child who is being pressured, pushed, and exploited by adults. Chapter 6 explains the differences between being an advocate for your child and being a pushy parent.

Rule 6: Consult with the "experts" about your child's developmental needs, and then use their input to become your own expert.

As the parent of a gifted child, it is inevitable that you will need some special parenting help. How much help is necessary will depend on your knowledge, education, and insight into the meaning of giftedness. It is always better to be more informed than underinformed. Try to gather as much information as possible in areas that concern you. Make your own decisions after reviewing the advice and information you receive from others. It can be dangerous to follow other people's rules. You know your child better than anyone else.

Rule 7: Find other parents, teachers, and relatives who support the challenges of raising a gifted child.

Having a support group that understands your challenges is crucial to your mental health and well being. Feedback from people who empathize with your problems or issues is very helpful to your decision making. This rule is explained in Chapters 1, 2, and 7. Conversely, you should ignore parents who tell you that raising a gifted child should be easier than raising a nongifted child.

Rule 8: Pay close attention to your child's social development.

Help your child create a meaningful and diverse social life. Just as your child's emotional intensity is something to be aware of, so, too, is how your child interacts with peers and adults socially. Don't leave social development to chance. You need to understand how your child feels about his or her interactions with others. Try and be sensitive to your child's sense of self socially. If you are aware, you are more likely to fend off problems with isolation or false self-adaptions—such as dumbing-down behavior to fit in. Chapters 4 and 7 address these social issues.

Rule 9: Communicate openly with your child and all members of the family.

Open communication is essential with your son or daughter. You should know how your children are feeling about school, friends, family life. Although it is not good to *force* your child to be open, it is very important to allow open dialogue to develop. Chapter 5 and Chapter 7 address the underlying issues involved in talking with your child about their feelings, thoughts, and issues.

Rule 10: Make careful decisions, always evaluate your plans, and be ready to revise them when necessary.

It is crucial to develop *your own vision* about the right way to raise your gifted child. You will naturally do this if you think through a careful plan about how you want to parent. Like all other important plans, your parenting plan will have to be revised along the way, because life is full of unexpected circumstances or events.

Conclusions

If you are able to use your independent thinking together with your emotional reactions, you will develop effective parenting strategies and skills. For example, when you are concerned about an issue related to your child's development, explore your concerns and try to resolve them through understanding and insight. When appropriate, you may need to take action.

Always remember, it helps to stay calm. It also is critical to let your child be his or her own person. When you put your dreams and expectations onto your sons or daughters you are robbing them of the chance to develop their personal sense of self and identity. When you maintain your own separate life goals outside of being a good enough parent, you are more likely to avoid the common parenting traps that gifted children unknowingly set up.

Selected References

Bloom, B. (ed.) (1985). *Developing Talent in Young People*. New York: Ballantine Books.

Clark, B. (2002). *Growing Up Gifted*. (6th ed). Columbus, OH: Merrill/ Prentice Hall.

Colangelo, N. (1991, 1997, 2003). "Counseling Gifted Students." In *Handbook of Gifted Education*, ed. By Nichols Colangelo and Gary A. Davis. Boston: Allyn and Bacon.

Colangelo, N., and P. Brower (1987). "Labeling Gifted Youngsters: Long–Term Impact on Families." *Gifted Child Quarterly, 31*, 75–78.

Colangelo, N., and D. F. Dettmann (1983). "A Review of Research on Parents and Families of Gifted Children." *Exceptional Children 50(1)*: 20–27.

Colangelo, N., and C. Fleuridas (1986). "The Abdication of Childhood: Special Issue: Counseling the Gifted and Talented." *Journal of Counseling Development, 64(9),* 561–563.

Cross, T. L. (2004). "The Rage of Gifted Students." In T. Cross (ed.), *On the Social and Emotional Lives of Gifted Children: Issues and Factors in Their Psychological Development* (2nd ed., pp. 109–114). Waco, TX: Prufrock Press.

Dabrowski, K., and M. M. Piechowski (1977). *Theory of Levels of Emotional Development* (vol. 1). Oceanside, NY: Dabor Science.

Davidson, J., and B. Davidson, (2004). *Genius Denied: How to Stop Wasting Our Brightest Young Minds*. New York: Simon & Schuster.

Davis, G. A., and S. Rimm (1985). *Education of the Gifted and Talented*. Engelwood Cliffs, NJ: Prentice–Hall.

Delisle, J. R. (1986). "Death with Honors: Suicide Among Gifted Adolescents." *Journal of Counseling and Development, 64,* 558–560.

Gagné, F. (1991). "Toward a Differentiated Model of Giftedness and Talent." In N. Colangelo & G.A. Davis (eds.), *Handbook of Gifted Education* (pp. 65–80). Boston: Allyn & Bacon.

Gagné, F. (1995). "Hidden Meaning of the 'Talent Development' Concept." *Educational Forum, 59*(4), 349–362.

Gardner, H. (1983). *Frames of Mind: The Theory of Multiple Intelligences.* New York: Basic Books.

Gardner, H. (1993a). *Frames of Mind: The Theory of Multiple Intelligences,* 10th ed. New York: Basic Books.

Gardner, H. (1993b). *Multiple Intelligences: The Theory in Practice.* New York: Basic Books.

Gardner, H. (1997). *Extraordinary Minds, Masterminds.* New York: Basic Books.

Gardner, H., and C. Wolf (1988). "The Fruits of Asynchrony: Creativity from a Psychological Point of View." *Adolescent Psychiatry, 15,* 106–123.

Halsted, J. W. (2002). *Some of My Best Friends Are Books: Guiding Gifted Readers from Preschool Through High School* (2nd ed.). Scottsdale, AZ: Great Potential Press.

Kerr, B. A. (1997). *Smart Girls: A New Psychology of Girls, Women, and Giftedness.* Scottsdale, AZ: Great Potential Press.

Kerr, B. A. (2001). *Smart Boys: Giftedness, Manhood, and the Search for Meaning.* Scottsdale, AZ: Great Potential Press.

Miller, A. (1996). *The Drama of the Gifted Child: The Search for the True Self* (rev. ed). New York: Basic Books.

Neihart, M. (1999). "The Impact of Giftedness on Psychological Well-Being: What Does the Empirical Literature Say?" *Roeper Review, 22(1),* 10–17.

Neihart, M. (2000). "Gifted Children with Asperger's Syndrome." *Gifted Child Quarterly, 44(4),* 222–230.

Neihart, M., et al., eds. (2002) *The Social and Emotional Development of Gifted Children: What Do We Know?* Waco, TX: Prufock Press.

Olenchak, F. R. (1994). "Talent Development." *The Journal of Secondary Gifted Education, 5(3),* 40–52.

Piechowski, M. (1991). "Emotional Development and Emotional Giftedness." In N. Colangelo and G.A. Davis (Eds.), *Handbook of Gifted Education* (285–306). Boston: Allyn & Bacon.

Renzulli, J. S. (1986a). *Systems and Models for Developing Programs for the Gifted and Talented.* Mansfield Center, CT: Creative Learning Press.

Rimm, S. (1988). "Family Environments of Underachievement of Gifted Students: What Do We Know and Where Do We Go?" *Gifted Child Quarterly 32(4):* 353–95.

Rimm, S. B. (1995). *Why Bright Kids Get Poor Grades: And What You Can Do About It.* New York: Crown.

Rivero, L. (2002). *Creative Home Schooling: A Resource for Smart Families.* Scottsdale, AZ: Great Potential Press.

Roeper, A. (1995). *Selected Writing and Speeches.* Minneapolis, MN: Free Spirit.

Seligman, M. E. P. (1995). *The Optimistic Child: A Proven Program to Safeguard Children Against Depression and Build Lifelong Resilience.* New York: Harper Collins.

Silverman, L. K. (1988). "The Second Child Syndrome." *Mensa Bulletin, 320:* 18–120.

Silverman, L. K. (1993). *Counseling the Gifted and Talented.* Denver, CO: Love.

Silverman, L. K. (1993). "The Gifted Individual." In L. Silverman (Ed.), *Counseling the Gifted and Talented* (1st ed., pp. 3–28). Denver, CO: Love.

Silverman, L. K. (1997). "The Construct of Asynchronous Development." *Peabody Journal of Education, 72(3–4),* 36–58.

Silverman, L., and K. Kearney (1989). "Parents of the Extraordinarily Gifted." *Advanced Development Journal* I (January): 41–56.

Silverman, L., and L. Leviton. (1991). "Advice to Parents in Search of the Perfect Program." *Gifted Child Today 14(6):* 31–34.

Smutney, J. F. (2001). *Stand Up for Your Gifted Child: How to Make the Most of Kids' Strengths at School and at Home.* Minneapolis, MN: Free Spirit Publishing.

Sternberg, R. (1985). "Critical Thinking: Its Nature, Measurement, and Improvement." In *Essays on the Intellect,* ed. By Frances R Link. Alexandria, VA: Association for Supervision and Curriculum Development: 45–65.

Sternberg, R., ed. (1999). *Handbook of Creativity.* Cambridge, Eng.: Cambridge University Press.

Sternberg, R. J., and J. E. Davidson (eds.). (1986). *Conceptions of Giftedness.* Cambridge: Cambridge University Press.

Streznewski, M. K. (1999). *Gifted Grown–ups: The Mixed Blessings of Extraordinary Potential.* New York: Wiley & Sons.

Tolan, S. *Is It a Cheetah?* (online). Hollingworth Center, 1997 (cired 29 May 2002). Available at http://www/ditd.org/cybersource/record .aspx?sid=11469&scat=902&stype=110

Tucker, B., and N. L. Hafenstein (1997). "Psychological Intensities in Young Gifted Children." *Gifted Child Quarterly, 41(3): 66–75.*

Webb, J. T., and A. R. DeVries (1998). *Gifted Parent Groups: The SENG Model.* Scottsdale, AZ: Great Potential Press.

Winner, E. (1997). "Exceptionally High Intelligence and Schooling." *American Psychologist 52*: 1070–1081.

Suggested Reading

Davidson, J., and B. Davidson, (2004). *Genius Denied: How to Stop Wasting Our Brightest Young Minds*. New York: Simon & Schuster.

Goldman, L. (2004). *Raising Our Children to Be Resilient: A Guide to Helping Children Cope with Trauma in Today's World*. New York: Brunner–Routledge.

Lerner, S. (2005). *Kids Who Think Outside the Box*. New York: Amacom.

Levine, M. (2003). *A Mind at a Time: America's Top Learning Expert Shows How Every Child Can Succeed*. New York: Touchstone Books.

Lovecky, D. V. (2004). *Different Minds: Gifted Children with AD/HD, Asperger Syndrome, and other Learning Deficits*. London: Jessica Kingsley.

Olenchak, F. R. (1998). *They Say My Kid's Gifted: Now What?* Waco, TX: Prufrock Press.

Ruf, Deborah. *Losing Our Minds: Gifted Children Left Behind*. Scottsdale, AZ: Great Potential Press.

Sayler, M. (1997). *Raising Champions: A Parent Handbook for Nurturing Gifted Children*. Waco, TX: Prufrock Press.

Webb, J. T., Amend, E. R., Webb, N. E., et al. (2005). *Misdiagnosis and Dual Diagnoses of Gifted Children and Adults: ADHD, Bipolar, OCD, Asperger's, Depression, and Other Disorders*. Scottsdale, AZ: Great Potential Press.

Webb, J. T., Meckstroth, E. A., and Tolan S. S. (contributor) (1989). *Guiding the Gifted Child: A Practical Source for Parents and Teachers*. Scottsdale, AZ: Great Potential Press.

Winner, E. (1997). *Gifted Children: Myths and Realities.* New York: Basic Books.

Yahnke Walker, S., and S. K. Perry (2002). *The Survival Guide for Parents of Gifted Kids: How to Understand, Live With, and Stick Up for Your Gifted Child.* Minneapolis, MN: Free Spirit Publishing.

Index

ability, 3, 12, 15, 22, 36, 43, 46, 81,
    86, 98, 104, 109, 110, 113, 122,
    134, 162, 188, 192
academic, 3–5, 36, 44, 45, 50, 52,
    77, 85–86, 91, 93, 96–97, 131,
    174–175, 177, 180, 183, 190,
    91, 193, 195
acceleration, 44, 74–76, 87, 95,
    101–102, 107, 133, 175, 177,
    178, 181
acceptance, 7, 34, 36, 38, 58–60,
    111, 120, 125, 127, 135,
    143–145, 154, 157, 168, 203,
    208, 211–213
accessory parents, 10, 19–22, 24–25,
    30, 38
acting older, 134–135, 159
acting out, 4, 133, 157
actualization, 1, 181–182
advocate, 8, 17, 131, 138, 172, 198,
    217–218, 223–224
anti-intellectual bias, 2, 8
anxiety, anticipatory, 124, 162
anxiety, parental, 30, 108, 113, 155,
    222
anxiety, separation, 9, 110, 123–124,
    156
anxiety, situational, 98, 119,
    123–124, 162

anxiety, social, 9, 16, 151–153,
    173–174
anxious, 52, 68, 85
appropriate parenting, 1–2, 109
argumentativeness, 140–141
arguments, 157, 210
ask yourself questions, 39, 162, 198,
    201
Asperger's Syndrome, 37, 45
assessment, 15, 81, 105, 172, 175,
    196
asynchronous development, 88, 95,
    128, 130
attention, 1, 26, 41, 52–55, 58,
    77, 81, 94, 95, 97, 99, 109,
    111, 117, 136, 140, 145,
    148, 154, 157, 159, 160,
    170, 173, 183–184, 193, 194,
    199, 201–203, 207, 211, 215,
    224
attention deficit, 81, 97, 163
attitude, 114, 190, 219
authority, 105, 115, 136, 145,
    160–161, 165, 202, 212
availability, 160

balance, 110–111, 127, 191, 195,
    200, 201, 203, 205, 206, 208,
    210, 219